Song of a Wounded Heart

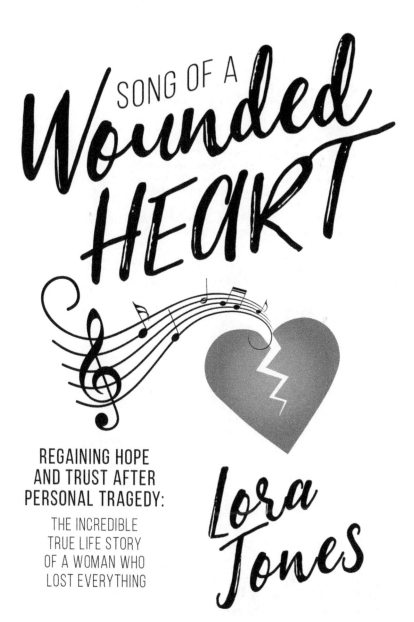

SONG OF A Wounded HEART

REGAINING HOPE AND TRUST AFTER PERSONAL TRAGEDY:

THE INCREDIBLE TRUE LIFE STORY OF A WOMAN WHO LOST EVERYTHING

Lora Jones

M·J

NASHVILLE

NEW YORK • LONDON • MELBOURNE • VANCOUVER

Song of a Wounded Heart

Regaining Hope and Trust After Personal Tragedy : The Incredible True Life Story of a Woman Who Lost Everything

© 2019 Lora Jones

All rights reserved. No portion of this book may be reproduced, stored in a retrieval system, or transmitted in any form or by any means—electronic, mechanical, photocopy, recording, scanning, or other—except for brief quotations in critical reviews or articles, without the prior written permission of the publisher.

Published in New York, New York, by Morgan James Publishing. Morgan James is a trademark of Morgan James, LLC. www.MorganJamesPublishing.com

ISBN 9781642792201 paperback
ISBN 9781642792218 eBook
Library of Congress Control Number: 2018909115

Cover and Interior Design by:
Chris Treccani
www.3dogcreative.net

Morgan James Publishing Builds with... Habitat for Humanity® Peninsula and Greater Williamsburg

Morgan James is a proud partner of Habitat for Humanity Peninsula and Greater Williamsburg. Partners in building since 2006.

Get involved today! Visit
MorganJamesPublishing.com/giving-back

Credits

Scripture quotations are from The Holy Bible, New International Version. Copyright © 1973, 1978, 1984 by International Bible Society.

Lyrics quoted from "Voice Of Truth" words and music by Mark Hall and Steven Curtis Chapman, from Casting Crown's 2003 debut album, *Casting Crowns*. Copyright © 2003

Sparrow Song (BMI) My Refuge Music (BMI) (adm. at CapitolCMGPublishing.com) / Peach Hill Songs (BMI) / Be Essential Songs (BMI) All rights reserved. Used by permission.

Be Essential Songs (BMI) / (admin at EssentialMusicPublishing.com). All rights reserved. Used by permission.

MY REFUGE MUSIC (BMI), SPARROW SONG (BMI), BMG RIGHTS MANAGEMENT (UK) LTD. (PRS), ONE BLUE PETAL MUSIC and SONY/ATV MUSIC PUBLISHING LLC (BMI)

MY REFUGE MUSIC and SPARROW SONG Admin. at CAPITOLCMGPUBLISHING.COM

BMG RIGHTS MANAGEMENT (UK) LTD. and ONE BLUE PETAL MUSIC Admin. by BMG RIGHTS MANAGEMENT (US) LLC

SONY/ATV MUSIC PUBLISHING LLC Admin. by SONY/ATV MUSIC PUBLISHING LLC, 424 Church Street, Suite 1200, Nashville, TN 37219 All rights reserved. Used by permission. Reprinted by permission of Hal Leonard LLC

Lyrics quoted from "How Great Thou Art," by Stuart K. Hine. Copyright © 1949, 1953 The Stuart Hine Trust CIO. All rights in the USA its territories and possessions, except print rights, administered by Capitol CMG Publishing. USA, North and Central American print rights and all Canadian and South American rights administered by Hope Publishing Company. All other North and Central American rights administered by the Stuart Hine Trust CIO. Rest of the world rights administered by Integrity Music Europe. All rights reserved. Used by permission.

Lyrics quoted from "Homesick," by Bart Millard, from MercyMe 2004 *Undone* album. Copyright © 2004 Simpleville Music (ASCAP) / (admin at EssentialMusicPublishing.com). All rights reserved. Used by permission.

Lyrics quoted from "Blessed Be Your Name," by Beth Redman and Matt Redman, from the 2005 album *Blessed Be Your Name—The Songs of Matt Redman, Volume 1*. Copyright © 2002 Thankyou Music (PRS) (adm. worldwide at CapitolCMGPublishing.com excluding Europe which is adm. by Integrity Music, part of the David C Cook family. Songs@integritymusic.com) All rights reserved. Used by permission.

Lyrics quoted from "Untitled Hymn," by Chris Rice, from 2003 album *Run the Earth, Watch the Sky*. Words and Music by Chris Rice. Copyright ©2003 Clumsy Fly Music (ASCAP). All rights administered by WB Music Corp. Used by permission.

Lyrics quoted from "If You Want Me To," by Ginny Owens and Kyle David Matthews, from the 1999 album *Without Condition* by Ginny Owens. Copyright © 1999 Universal Music—Brentwood Benson Publ. (ASCAP) (adm. at CapitolCMGPublishing.com) All rights reserved. Used by permission.

Lyrics quoted from "The Church Triumphant," by Gloria Gaither and William J. Gaither, from the 2009 album *Reunited* by Gaither Vocal Band. Copyright © 1973 Hanna Street Music (BMI) (adm. at CapitolCMGPublishing.com) All rights reserved. Used by permission.

Lyrics quoted from "Unaware." Words and Music by Peter Kipley, Mike Scheuchzer, Robby Shaffer, Jim Bryson, Bart Millard, Barry E. Graul and Nathan Cochran , from the 2004 album *Undone* by MercyMe. Copyright © 2004 Wordspring Music LLC (SESAC) and Songs From the Indigo Room (SESAC). All rights on behalf of Wordspring Music LLC and Songs From the Indigo Room administered by W.B.M. Music Corp. Used by permission.

Simpleville Music (ASCAP) / Wet As A Fish Music (ASCAP) / (admin at EssentialMusicPublishing.com). All rights reserved. Used by permission.

Lyrics quoted from "Who Am I," by John Mark Hall, from Casting Crown's 2003 debut album *Casting Crowns*. Copyright © 2003 My Refuge Music (BMI) (adm. at CapitolCMGPublishing.com) / Be Essential Songs (BMI). All rights reserved. Used by permission. Be Essential Songs (BMI) / (admin at EssentialMusicPublishing.com). All rights reserved. Used by permission.

Lyrics quoted from "Lifesong," by John Mark Hall, from the 2005 album *Lifesong* by Casting Crowns. Copyright © 2005 My Refuge Music (BMI) (adm. at CapitolCMGPublishing.com) / Be Essential Songs (BMI) All rights reserved. Used by permission. Be Essential Songs (BMI) / (admin at EssentialMusicPublishing.com). All rights reserved. Used with permission.

Lyrics quoted from "I'm With You (Ruth and Naomi)," by Bernie Herms and Nichole Nordeman, from the 2011 album Music Inspired by the Story by various artists. Vocals by Nichole Nordeman and Amy Grant. Copyright © 2011 Capitol CMG Paragon (BMI) Birdwing Music (ASCAP) Birdboy Songs (ASCAP) Bernie Herms Music (BMI) (adm. at CapitolCMGPublishing.com) All rights reserved. Used by permission.

Poem entitled "Faith" quoted from *The Leaning Tree* by Patrick Overton. Copyright © 1975 by Bethany Press, St. Louis, Missouri. All rights reserved. Used by permission. Poem reprinted in *Rebuilding the Front Porch of America: Essays on the Art of Community Making*. Bitterroot Mountain Publishing, 1997 and 2017. All rights reserved. Used by permission.

For my four Js:

Jesus, J. L., Janessa, and Jayden

Table of Contents

Preface

It's taken a village to write this book. Many walked with me through this process, lending me their skills. I wrestled, cried, laughed, and remembered as I wrote it. When I neared its completion, I read it to my dear Momma just weeks before she passed from this earthly life to glory. I became a little braver when she said, "Good job."

Now it's in your hands.

My heart lays vulnerable on these pages.

Here I tell God's story of my life. May He use it in His story of *your* life. Mine is not any more important than yours. Whether we write a book or not, our lives are treasured by God, nonetheless.

I pray as you read, God will speak, and you will have the courage to "*listen and believe the Voice of Truth.*"[1]

Part I
THE NIGHT GOD SANG

Chapter 1
SUDDEN GOODBYES

"By day the Lord directs his love,
at night his song is with me . . ."

PSALM 42:8

November 23, 2004

Our kids didn't bother to grab jackets when they left the house that morning. The sun peeked through scattered clouds as I watched them from our front porch. It was the Tuesday before Thanksgiving and it promised to be a comfortable, cloudy sixty-degree day. Only an occasional stray raindrop found its way to the earth. Perfect traveling weather.

But a cool breeze whispered the coming of winter.

I glanced at the time and hurried inside to pack our suitcases and the hand-crafted snowmen I'd made for early Christmas gifts. Seated in his home office chair nearby, J. L. spoke by phone with a layperson who'd be leading a meeting in his absence. "You can do it without me," he said with a smile. Hanging up the phone, J. L. turned to his computer to write one last e-mail before our trip. Concern etched his forehead as he typed a heartfelt prayer for a close friend. We both had lots to do before school released. Then we'd hit the road for Kansas.

The ministry had brought us to this busy little town in the far corner of Northeastern Oklahoma—Miami to be exact—pronounced [My-am-uh] by the natives. My husband, J. L., served as pastor of Immanuel Baptist Church, a congregation of about 125. "Learn to pronounce it right so everyone knows you belong," one church member suggested when we first arrived.

Excited to become acquainted with us, our new friends at church asked the same curious question J. L. received throughout his life. "What's your full name?" someone asked.

Since J. L. *was* his full name, I enjoyed listening to his comical answers. He usually chose a silly name and waited to see if they believed him. His mischievous eyes always gave him away. If not, J. L.'s contagious laughter soon eased the embarrassment of the gullible ones. Everyone loved his good-natured sense of humor. He was soon nicknamed Pastor J.

We'd had mixed emotions about moving from Grand Island, Nebraska, to Miami, Oklahoma. J. looked forward in anticipation for a place to try some innovative ideas. I hoped to be more involved with the children's school. Jayden thought of it as a great adventure. His green eyes sparkled with excitement and a bit of mischievousness, like his father. "We'll make new friends, sissy," he encouraged his sister, Janessa. Pushing her long, blonde hair behind one ear, she said, "I'll try," but quietly vowed to move back to Nebraska for college with her friends. Her heart already ached with the anticipation of loneliness.

When we got to Miami, we all fell in love with the area and its people right away. "It's amazing to live where God planted the trees," my husband said.

Miami is right at the western edge of the Ozarks where plentiful rain allows trees, flowers, and grass to grow in abundance—nothing like the high desert plains of Liberal, Kansas, where our extended families lived. Even though others discount Southwest Kansas, it's always been beautiful to me. At dusk, the fingertips of God paint the magnificent colors of a glorious sunset that gives way to the amazing starlit nights on the open prairie.

Kansas would always be home to me.

By the time we'd been in Miami for four years, friends surrounded Janessa, exactly as her brother had predicted before the move. A happy extrovert, she delighted in being with people and loved to be on the go. My momma-heart worried about coping with the upcoming changes in her. Her friends were becoming more important than her family, and I missed how my girl used to crawl in my lap to snuggle with me. Her friends needed her though, with her say-it-as-it-is attitude. They trusted her advice and asked for it often.

Our eleven-year-old son, Jayden, entered middle school that fall. Our church youth group included sixth graders, much to Janessa's chagrin. Jayden loved his sissy and wanted to follow her everywhere. It frustrated her when her friends wanted him to tag along. They loved her little brother. He brightened a room with his smile and easy laughter. Smart as a whip, he processed thoughts much faster than me, but he wasn't vain about his intellect. Instead of being arrogant, he empathized with the pain of others. Often J. and Janessa teased Jayden and I for tearing up when we watched movies together.

GOING HOME

That afternoon J. and I drove to pick up the kids from school. I watched them bound across the school yard. The van jiggled when they tossed their bookbags behind them and buckled their seatbelts. The happy chaos of competing voices filled the van. J. and I grinned at each other and settled in for the lengthy, 400-mile drive.

Because J.'s duties at the church often kept us from traveling home for Christmas, our tradition was to travel to our parents' homes in November. This year, we planned to celebrate Christmas early with my family, then spend Thanksgiving with J.'s family.

By the time we crossed the Oklahoma-Kansas border, the pitter-pat on the windshield had become a steady sound. We drove in rain for a few hours, then stopped for a late supper in Wichita, Kansas, where J.'s younger brother, Jack, and his family met us for pizza. Jack and Kris's two preschool children loved their Uncle J. He had the whole family laughing at his antics, playing with the little ones as we ate our fill of pizza.

I'll never forget how J. stood the baby in the middle of the table and played with him until he kicked someone's soda, splashing it everywhere. We laughed while we cleaned up the mess together. With that same mischievous grin, Jack teased J. about getting everyone into trouble.

We left the restaurant around 9:00 p.m., urged on by the weather forecast of snow coming across the plains, and the lateness of the evening. The bite of the cold wind made us grateful to pull on the winter coats packed in the van.

As we snuggled into our seats, I called ahead to check on my mom and the farmhouse.

The natural gas well on her land was receiving routine maintenance by the company who drilled the well and sold the gas. They provided the utilities for Mom's house as a benefit to the landowner but forgot to consider that fact when they scheduled the job. When they shut the well down to make their scheduled updates, it inadvertently left Mom without heat and hot water for several days. I was hoping for good news.

"Do you have gas?" I asked my mother.

J. chuckled and asked, "Isn't that a personal question?"

Giggles rippled through the van and over the phone. The levity J. brought to the moment helped relieve my frustration. The complication hadn't rattled my eighty-year-old mom in the least. She said she was using electric heaters to heat the house and warming water for bathing in the microwave.

"Lora, you might rather stay at J.'s parents' house first, so you can shower. They should have our gas back on in a few days."

Mom's calm temperament amazed me.

Given the circumstances, we decided to stay with J.'s parents the first couple of days of our trip. When I hung up, I called Mom Jones to tell her about the change in plans and let her know to expect us shortly after midnight.

As the temperature continued to drop, the rain changed to snow. The kids giggled with each other in the backseat. I loved how they played together, particularly on our family trips. At home, friends from school or the neighborhood came to play. In front of her friends,

Janessa pretended her brother annoyed her—well, maybe he really did annoy her. At fourteen, girls are annoyed with almost everything.

Tonight, with no one else around, she let herself enjoy the company of her younger brother. To the sweet sounds of their laughter, I fell asleep.

To the sweet sounds of their laughter, I fell asleep.

I expected to wake up in Liberal.

SHOCK

I awoke from my sleep because lights shone directly in my face for a moment. I seemed to drift to sleep again, and when I awoke, I couldn't take a breath.

What in the world is wrong with me? I thought. *I have to make noise, so J. knows I can't breathe.*

I opened my mouth, but no sound came out. Frustrated and confused, I opened my eyes to a hazy fog. The strange, wheezy sound of my own first breath echoed in my ears.

As my eyes cleared, the passenger door opened, and I instinctively tried to get out of the van. I put my feet out the door and tried to raise myself up, but dizziness overtook me. A tremendous pain shot through my chest.

Then I heard a woman's fearful voice agonize, "Oh no, oh no, oh no!"

What's wrong?

Unable to continue sitting up, I leaned against something with my feet out the door. It didn't occur to me there shouldn't have been anything to lean on there, in between the front seats. Slowly, I moved my eyes and head to look around.

Finally, I understood.

We've been in an accident.

J. sat beside me to my right, more in the center of the van than the driver's seat should be. I reached for him, held his face in my hands, and whispered, "Wake up, sweetheart."

Suddenly, I froze in fear. What if I harmed him by the small movement of taking his face in my hands? I determined to hold his head securely, and not move.

My whispers became pleas. I begged J. to open his eyes. Air escaped from his lips, giving me hope he would soon wake up.

But he didn't.

Time seemed to stop while I continued to hold J.'s head, unwilling to let go.

My eyes searched the backseat. There, still buckled into the seat, sat my precious Janessa. She, too, appeared to be sleeping. People surrounded her, working to stabilize her into a neck brace.

I couldn't see Jayden from my position, but I could hear people behind J.'s seat. Then someone said, "We have a faint heartbeat."

He's alive. God help us. Please, please help us.

EMTs seemed to be everywhere. Voices asked me questions, and I tried to answer loud enough to be heard. It hurt so much just to breathe.

In the middle of the chaos, a soothing voice began to sing. It calmed my spirit when I focused on the words. I listened intently, convinced the voice came from God Himself. The melody He sang seemed familiar. Maybe I listened to it on the radio in earlier weeks. I didn't remember the lyrics on my own, but now the first four words sounded rich and clear.

"Do not be afraid,"[2] God sang.

Afraid? I'm terrified! Help us, God, please help us.

"Do not be afraid."[3] The record seemed to be stuck. Over and over the song repeated itself. His gentle voice sang the tender command. It reminded me of the way J. spoke to the kids when he'd taught them how to swim. To keep them from panicking, he often said, "I've got you, don't fight me."

I felt like God said, "I've got you, don't panic."

So I watched people care for my children, answered the questions of the EMTs, and listened to the song, while holding tightly to the hope that J. would soon start breathing again.

Someone came to my feet and leaned into the van. In a voice heavy with emotion, he said to me, "This is going to be hard. You are going to have to be strong." He introduced himself as the hospital chaplain. He'd been a few cars behind us when the accident occurred and arrived at the scene along with the first responders. His quiet, confident presence helped me maintain my grip on hope. Somehow, I found the breath to give him our emergency contact numbers. He promised to call them.

An unknown amount of time slipped by unnoticed. I jabbered to J., Janessa, and Jayden—or at least I think I spoke aloud. Shallow breathing made it difficult, but I longed to tell each of them how much I loved them.

I asked the faceless voices around me, "Are we alive?

"We are working on it," they assured me.

"Will someone help my husband?" I asked.

I heard someone say, "Yes," but no one hovered around him in the same way they carefully monitored the rest of us. It should have been a clue to my mind.

As time passed, I caught longer pieces of the song, and its message sank deeper into my heart. The words seemed very important to hear. Each phrase of the song came when I needed it and gave me a moment of clarity. Phrase by phrase, note by note, God sang the song to me, making sure each word clearly spoke to me.

"The voice of truth says, 'This is for My glory,'"[4] God sang.

For Your glory? Okay, You are doing something here. Something is going to change.

I didn't understand, and I didn't try to figure it out. Instead, the song brought a strange, out-of-place comfort in the middle of paralyzing fear.

"We will take you to the ambulance first," an EMT told me.

Why? Don't the others need more help than me?

I hesitated because I still held J.'s head. I didn't want to hurt him by putting his head down. Someone reached through his window and said, "I'll hold him for you."

When I saw that hands held him securely, I finally let go. Technicians put me on a backboard and into an ambulance.

Wheeled away by paramedics into the dark night, a convulsion of shivers overtook me, but it wasn't from the cold. The shivering came from deep within my soul.

... a convulsion of shivers overtook me, but it wasn't from the cold. The shivering came from deep within my soul.

Shock, I later learned.

A much too simple word to describe the horror of the night.

STAY AWAKE

My bewildered mind tried to reconcile the events of the evening as I lay on the backboard on a gurney in the emergency room. I tried to think clearly, but it took concentration to simply inhale. Breathing hurt—terribly. I ached to move, but the backboard held me captive. At the same time, dizziness led to overwhelming nausea.

Fear trumped everything.

In desperation, I clung to the song. "Do not be afraid."[5]

God, please help us. Fix it.

I felt the tender touch of the nurses. One of them voiced a prayer over me.

The emergency room became silent when the chaplain arrived. He took a deep breath, reached out, and touched my feet. "I called your brother, your husband's family, and your church family, and now that they know, I need to tell you. Your husband and your son did not survive the accident. We don't expect your daughter to live through the night."

"Out of all the voices calling out to me, I will choose to listen and believe the voice of truth."[6] The song whispered in my head.

The chaplain explained that Janessa had been taken by another ambulance to Via Christi Trauma Center in Wichita. He had spoken with the doctors there and would continue to monitor their progress as they attempted to save her life. They didn't offer much hope, however. The nurses explained that an ambulance was en route to take me to Via Christi as well. They were unsure of my injuries and wanted further testing at the trauma center before they removed me from the backboard.

My eyes opened wide. Words crowded my mind in an incessant string of disconnected thoughts.

This must be a bad dream. Surely, I'll awake soon.

They didn't survive.

There must be some mistake. They must be wrong.

Janessa won't live through the night? She has to!

Any moment now, my family will just wake up and walk in.

How can I possibly survive?

Why did I survive?

I don't want to survive.

You are singing, God. I hear you.

The chaplain moved on to talk to another patient. In the next few moments, God gave me the opportunity to listen to him talk with the man behind the curtain. In the same tender voice, he spoke again, this time to the driver of the other vehicle. When I heard his response, I realized he felt responsible for our deaths. He wailed in mourning. "Why not me?" he called out in agony to God. The sound of his voice declared the terror in his soul.

I'll never, ever forget the sound. In that moment, unknown to him and to me, our God knit my heart to his.

God, how will either one of us survive?

It seemed we waited for an eternity for the ambulance—each in our own bed, separated by a curtain—each trapped in our own nightmare.

When the ambulance arrived, the team whisked us into the back, one on either side of a busy EMT who tried to help us both at the same time. The other driver cried out in agonizing pain, and the EMT worked to help him endure the ride. I hurt too, but nausea was my urgent problem. The backboard firmly held me immobile. Because I couldn't turn my head, nor move my arms, my own vomit went into my nose and smothered me, and I couldn't help myself. The EMT rescued me each time and pushed the puke from my nose.

"Mrs. Jones, I need you to stay awake," he said.

You mean I can go to sleep and not wake up?

I closed my eyes again and willed myself to sleep. But the vomiting woke me repeatedly. In an odd sort of struggle, I instinctively tried to gasp for breath and life, and then purposefully tried to fall asleep and grasp death.

J., I begged, *please don't leave me behind.*

HEAVEN'S VOICE

As soon as we arrived at Via Christi, people moved very quickly. Technicians x-rayed me again and told me they saw no broken bones. In mere moments, they released me from the prison of that backboard.

Again, a man appeared at my feet. "Your daughter has taken a turn for the worse. Do you want to see her?"

I could only nod.

Someone wheeled the gurney I was on down a hallway to the door of Janessa's room. A woman's voice called me by name, but I wasn't wearing my glasses—I couldn't tell who it was. I asked for my glasses and someone handed them to me. With them on, I recognized Emily, my nephew Darren's wife, beside me. She gently helped me into a wheelchair and rolled me into the room to see Janessa.

Time stopped and concern for pain or nausea completely left my mind.

Janessa laid on a bed in the center of the room. A single, thin sheet partially covered her swollen, still body. The only sounds came from a man at the head of her bed manually squeezing a bag of air into her lungs, slowly and steadily. My brother-in-law Jack and his wife, Kris, both so cheerful just hours before at the pizza parlor were inside the room with tear-stained faces. Darren and Emily stood close by as I absorbed the scene before me.

Time stopped and concern for pain or nausea completely left my mind.

Jack knelt beside my wheelchair. Kindness and strength emanated from him. He said to me, "She needs to go be with her daddy and her brother. But they need your permission to quit trying to keep her here."

I nodded, trying to comprehend what he was saying.

Emily knelt beside me on the other side and quietly explained what procedures the doctors had tried in an effort to save Janessa's life. They performed surgery to attempt to relieve the pressure on her brain. Nothing had worked. They could do nothing more.

Incongruously, I thought, *I can't take that man home with me to breathe for her.*

I swallowed hard.

In their kindness, they'd kept her breathing until I arrived. Everything paused and waited for my instructions, except the man with his breathing bag.

I nodded permission. They pushed my wheelchair to her bedside, and my family clustered around us. I took her hand and whispered, "I'll be okay sweetheart, I love you. It's okay to go." The words caught in my throat.

During the quiet moments of goodbye, a voice began to sing. This time it was Emily. She sang the chorus of the classic Christian hymn "How Great Thou Art"[7]. We joined together for the last verse:

"When Christ shall come with shout of acclamation
and take me home—what joy shall fill my heart!
Then I shall bow in humble adoration,
And there proclaim, My God how great thou art!
Then sings my soul, my Savior God, to thee,
How great thou art! How great thou art!
Then sings my soul, my Savior God, to thee,
How great thou art! How great thou art!"[8]

Janessa never took a breath on her own. Her heart slowly stopped beating. By the time our song completed, she safely arrived home in heaven, with her God, her daddy, and her bubba.

God help me.

Several years later, Emily and I talked together, reliving the details of the night. I wanted her to know how much it meant to me that she sang that song. Quietly, she confessed something. "I know my mouth was moving, but it wasn't me singing. It wasn't my voice, and

I couldn't sing that song without reading the lyrics." She'd pondered it through the years and wondered if an angel sang to us, or maybe Janessa, or even Jesus singing through her own voice. Unsure what others might think if she shared her thoughts, she'd kept it to herself.

The more I considered it, the more I became convinced God allowed us to listen in while Janessa entered heaven. The verse we sang is in first person, like Janessa had spoken the words herself. Every time I reflect on it, it takes my breath away. I envision her breaking into song, running through the gates of heaven, and twirling around in an attempt to drink in the glory of it all.

"When Christ shall come with shout of acclamation and take *me* home—what joy shall fill *my* heart!"[9] Janessa entered heaven singing.

"It was probably the most supernatural experience I have ever had," Emily told me recently. I agree. What a dramatic display of God's presence.

First, He proved Himself to be real by singing to me. Then, we heard my daughter exclaim her joy in song when she experienced the reality of God, face to face. The painful journey ahead stretched overwhelming and torturous, but the Bible says in Psalms 42:8, "By day the LORD directs his love, at night his song is with me . . ."

No matter how dark the night you are facing, I want you to know this: *He <u>is</u> real.*

Chapter 2
STEP BY STEP

"Whether you turn to the right or to the left, your ears will hear a voice behind you, saying, 'This is the way; walk in it.'"

ISAIAH 30:21

November 24, 2004

I lay in the lonely hospital room under thin blankets, silent with fear. I kept hoping a doctor would run in exclaiming, "They are alive! It's a miracle!" Yet when a small noise startled me, horrifying reality dissolved my daydream. My husband, my son, and my daughter were all dead. Once again, I closed my eyes and dared death to claim me too.

THE HAND OF GOD

Not even sleep could quiet my anxious thoughts or erase the vivid scenes of my memory. The truth relentlessly flooded my brain: I faced a future alone. My life had ended. My family had died—all of them.

What am I going to do?

A nurse tiptoed into the room. Silently she took me by the hand and led me like a dazed child into the bathroom. As we walked together, I caught a glimpse of a pitiful woman. It took a moment to realize it was my own reflection in a mirror. Dried vomit caused my shoulder-length hair to stick straight out from my head. My skin was ashen, and I was wearing a thin hospital gown.

My brain seemed to take a detour without my permission. Chuckling, I mumbled, "If Janessa sees me, she will die!" I imagined the look on her face if she saw my hair.

Suddenly, I jolted back to reality. Horrified by the terrible irony of my words, I wondered if the nurse heard me, and what she thought of me.

I must be losing my mind.

Little by little, the nurse cleaned me up and gently worked the mess out of my hair. Then she helped me crawl into bed.

My nephew, Darren, stayed with me the whole night. He'd grown up not far down the country road from us. During my high school years, he'd ridden his bike to play at our house. He was my little buddy, who grew up to be my friend.

Throughout the night, he frequently came to my bedside and checked on me. He stroked my hair, periodically peeling away pieces of the vomit still hiding there. His tender touch brought me comfort. He understood my pain. Only two years earlier, Darren and Emily had buried their first daughter.

Even with people around me who loved and cared for me, I felt lost and alone. Laying in the darkness, I cried out to God. Immediately it was like a blanket fell onto me. That blanket seemed to protect me and hold my heart together, at least for now. I curled up in it and hid in its comfort, afraid to move in the darkness.

Several weeks later, I realized the blanket was the hand of God, shielding me from the weight of the enormous pain to come.

DECISIONS

By daylight, I woke to the world swirling about me. I still felt dizzy and my mind refused to quiet. There were thousands of decisions to make, and I felt incapable of making a single one.

My dear brother-in-law Jack, came to my hospital room that morning. As a funeral director, he knew which decisions needed to be made right away—exactly the help I needed at that moment. He asked tough questions which required me to think and remember. *Where are the insurance policies? Should they be buried in Miami or Liberal? What about the place for the funeral?*

My mind flitted back to a random, unplanned conversation between J. and I. We'd found ourselves discussing where we wanted to be buried when we died.

"I suppose in Liberal, since it's our home base," J. had said. I agreed it made the most sense at this point in our lives.

"Would you marry again?" I asked tentatively.

"Absolutely!" he said with that ornery grin. He wrapped his arms around me. I nodded against his chest, knowing he'd need another partner if he lost me.

"What about you?" he asked, interrupting my thoughts.

"I doubt it," I said, and then the conversation went on to lighter and easier topics.

Nudged back to the present, I realized Jack was watching me, waiting for me to answer the questions.

"We'll bury them in Liberal," I said. One question down, a million more to go.

"But Miami and Liberal are 400 miles apart. It might be too far to travel for many who want to come." Jack commented. "What if we have two services?"

We decided to have the funeral service in Liberal, where my family would be buried and our parents lived, and a memorial service in Miami, where our church family and school family could celebrate their lives and mourn loss together.

As Jack and I made decisions, we waited for my brothers to arrive.

All three of my brothers and their wives were en route, bringing our mom with them. They'd delayed their drives to Wichita when they got the call the night before, so they could avoid the icy road conditions that caused our accident.

When they arrived, the hospital released me into Emily's care.

As a doctor, Emily knew what to watch for regarding my concussion and the shock I faced. I stayed with Emily and Darren at their house in Wichita. She helped me with the horrible nausea caused by the spinning in my head. I couldn't hold anything down until she gave me a patch to put behind my ear. That stopped the vertigo.

That first night I was too weak to feed myself, so Howard, my oldest brother, fed me supper that night. "It's been a long time since I fed you with a spoon," he said, gently reminding me that he was 18-years-old when I came along.

No one should ever have to pick out three caskets.

I slept beside my momma. No words helped—there was no way for either of us to fix it. But simply being together, knowing she understood, comforted me. I saw the mixture of past and present in her eyes. She still grieved the loss of her own son, over forty years ago, and her husband just a few years prior. The creases around her eyes showed the intensity of her concern for me. How could she help me bury my husband and both children at the same time?

No one should ever have to pick out three caskets.

After one night in Wichita, we caravanned to Liberal together where I stayed at my mom's house until the funeral. I'm sure we traveled there on Thanksgiving Day, but blocks of time are missing from my memory. Friends and family helped me with countless details in preparation for funeral number one to be held in Liberal on Saturday.

Jack was such a help to me during that time. He contacted the funeral homes, ordered caskets, talked to pastors, and helped gather the music. He even took care of his brother's body—literally preparing it for burial.

J.'s younger sister, Jana, and her husband, Mark, assembled pictures into a beautiful video for the funeral. They used the song God sang to me in the van, "Voice of Truth,"[10] for the background music.

When I listened to the rest of the lyrics, God astounded me with the words of the entire song. In that moment I felt they'd written the song specifically for me.

Whatever you do, don't stop singing, Father. That's how I am hearing your voice.

CROWDS OF PEOPLE

November 27, 2004

Nothing prepared me for the shock of seeing three hearses lined up in front of J.'s childhood church in Liberal, Kansas. Somehow it hadn't occurred to me that three caskets needed three hearses. The sight of them took my breath away.

When I remembered to breathe again, I looked around. The parking lot overflowed with cars. The church building swelled to capacity with people who loved J., Janessa, and Jayden. Step-by-step, my feet took me into the waiting area for the family. My heart pounded in my ears.

As the service began, I watched Jack and Jana, brother and sister, push their brother's casket down the aisle to the front of the church in a quiet demonstration of love. One by one, both families entered the sanctuary, forever connected by one amazing, godly man, J. L. Jones.

The sheer number of people astounded me. People came from both J.'s hometown church and mine, as well as from the churches J. pastored. Several carloads traveled the miles from Miami, Oklahoma, to say goodbye to their dear friend and pastor. Some even came from our church and neighborhood in Nebraska. Janessa's childhood friends cried with me, their future college plans with Janessa now forever changed. Family from across the country, high school friends from St. Louis, college friends from Houston, all gathered to honor my family. Hundreds of people came from far and wide to express their love. I cannot even begin to write a list, but sometimes, when I'm alone and quiet, I remember moments from the day God used His people to hold me up. I hugged as many as I could while protecting the broken rib on my left side. When we finally went back to Mom's house, I collapsed in exhaustion.

FOOTSTEPS OF JESUS

November 30, 2004

After the funeral, we focused on preparation for the memorial in Miami. I moved through the days in a fog. It felt surreal.

When Monday arrived, our family gathered once again to form a caravan across Kansas. This time, we headed east to Miami. Squinting into the sun, I looked out the windshield. The road stretched forward to the horizon, with no end in sight.

Just like the pain of my heart . . .

Lost in thought, I stared down the highway. When we entered a slight curve, the oncoming truck appeared to be heading straight into our lane. My body tensed, and I held my breath as the vehicle whizzed by in its own lane. Drawing a deep breath to slow my heartrate, I leaned back and closed my eyes. In a few minutes, I allowed exhaustion to take me into a peaceful sleep, away from the panic triggered by the sounds of the traffic.

In Miami on Tuesday morning, our families gathered once again for a funeral. This parking lot also overflowed with cars and trucks, the sidewalks crowded with people waiting to enter the sanctuary. We wondered if the church could hold all who wanted to attend.

The kids' school allowed students to attend the funeral if an adult came to get them from school. They released one hundred fifty students. At least 500 teenagers, parents, teachers, pastors, friends, congregants, and family crowded into every possible space in the precious church where J. pastored for four years. Nearly every room of the building filled with people. The church used video screens where possible and provided audio for the rest of the rooms.

Many of J.'s colleagues in the ministry attended. We honored these pastors by seating them in the choir loft. When our family came into the sanctuary, I blew them a kiss. I don't know why. It was my way of saying, "Thank you for being here for my husband, for sitting behind him today." In the days ahead, I needed their prayers and their strength to help me navigate the deep waters of grief.

This service differed from the one in Liberal in several ways. The pastor from our college days conducted the service. He knew us when we first fell in love and J. wholeheartedly surrendered to the ministry. He was able to share those stories at J.'s funeral.

The music reflected Janessa and Jayden's tastes. Their youth pastor had helped me find their favorite songs, and he organized a band to play them. While I listened to the music, I imagined them singing along.

Both of my children loved to sing. We teased Jayden because he always sang at the top of his lungs in the shower. After a lot of prodding, we finally convinced him to sing for church. Once he did so, he looked forward to performing again. Janessa, on the other hand, sang for church at three years old. She stopped singing publicly for a while during her preteen years, but when she became older, her voice strengthened, and her confidence grew. She dreamed of becoming a Christian recording artist.

Now I believe they both sing with their Daddy for the greatest of all audiences—the King Himself.

J. L. enjoyed singing too, although he didn't believe he sang well. He was wrong. I loved to listen to him sing. We even sang the old hymn "Footsteps of Jesus"[11] for our wedding, by recording it ahead of time. It was our promise to God.

"Sweetly, Lord, we have heard Thee calling, 'Come, follow me!'
And we see where Thy footprints falling, Lead us to thee.
Footprints of Jesus that make the pathway glow;
We will follow the steps of Jesus where'er they go."[12]

J. and I followed Jesus' footprints as closely as we could. They led us to minister to three churches in three states, preaching the good news of Jesus to all who would listen, until they led J. to the throne of God. Now, he rested at the feet of Jesus, but I had to find the footprints to follow from here. Alone.

A couple of days after the funeral, I sat in the recliner in my living room with a Bible on my lap, trying to read. The patch behind my ear helped me not be dizzy, but it caused my eyesight to be blurry. My sister-in-law Laura volunteered to read to me. I gratefully agreed.

She opened my Bible "randomly" and found an underlined passage. She read it aloud:

"How gracious he will be when you cry for help! As soon as he hears, he will answer you. Although the Lord gives you the bread of adversity and the water of affliction, your teachers will be hidden no more; with your own eyes you will see them. Whether you turn to the right or to the left, your ears will hear a voice behind you, saying, 'This is the way; walk in it'" (Isaiah 30:19b-21).

I pondered the verses and clung to the words of hope. Now more than ever, I needed God's voice to speak to me and to speak more clearly than I'd ever heard Him. The passage challenged me to trust God to do what He promised. Daily, sometimes hourly, I prayed:

What is your plan God? I have nothing left and I don't know what to do. These verses say you will tell me which way to go. I'm trusting you to do that. I'm so lost, so afraid, so alone. I'll do nothing until you tell me what to do. Help me hear you when you speak—or sing.

God heard my prayer.

FROM THE TRAUMA NURSE:

"I had only been a nurse for a little over a year on that night in November. It was a little before two in the morning when we got the call from the admissions desk that we were going to be getting a patient who had been in an accident. This was not uncommon as we were a med-surg trauma floor. I volunteered to take the patient since I had been there the longest (with the exception of the charge nurse) and I knew this case was going to be a tough one.

I remember the phone ringing and it was the ER nurse calling to give report and as I listened to her I could hardly hold it together. I got off the phone and immediately thought, "How am I going to do this?" The nurse had said they would bring Lora up as soon as she was done in the ER. Lora wanted to be with her daughter as she knew she was not going to make it. I knew I would have to hold it together for this woman when she got to our floor. The last thing she would need is a nurse blubbering all over her. But, I couldn't hold in the tears and I knew I needed prayer to be able to take care of this woman. I also knew that if this lady was going to get through this, she was going to need prayer, too.

So, I did what any good nurse would do; I went to the bathroom and broke down in a river of tears. As soon as I gained a little of my composure, I got my phone and called my mom (that is who you call at 2am when you need someone to pray for you). I remember my mom answering the phone and immediately she could tell something wasn't right. She calmly asked me what was wrong. I proceeded to tell her that I was about to get a patient who had just lost her whole family in a MVA (motor vehicle accident). As a nurse there are many rules involving confidentiality, but I thought it necessary to give Lora's first name so that my mom could have a name to put to her prayer. Little did Lora know that from the second she hit the door at St. Francis that night, someone was praying for her. Those prayers didn't stop that night . . . they continued for several years.

When Lora got to the floor, we rolled her into room 8047a (is that funny that even after this many years I still remember the room?) and moved her to the bed. I quickly assessed that she needed a shower as she had vomit in her hair. I quickly ran to get a new gown and the necessary materials for a shower then got her to the bathroom. I remember standing outside the tiny hospital shower picking vomit out of her hair (and getting sprayed by the showerhead that hit everything except what it needed to). I couldn't say anything; I was at a loss for words. So she sat and I stood in silence . . . me holding back tears as Lora sat in a state of shock (the look on her face spoke volumes). I got what I could out of her hair then helped her tie up her gown and put her back in bed.

I am a rule follower, but this night I decided it best not to bombard Lora with the many questions of the admission assessment. Instead, I filled out what I could and left the rest. By this time some of her family was there so I asked her if she needed anything (knowing full well what she needed I could not give to her). She said, "No," so I left in silence letting her know that if she did need anything to let me know. I checked on her several more times that night and each time she was sitting in silence with family. I left when my shift was over not knowing if I would ever see Lora again, but knowing that she would forever be in my thoughts and prayers.

My mom (whom I had called that night) perused the local newspaper a couple of days later to see if she could find Lora's last name and any more details about the accident that had taken place. She found that Lora was a pastor's wife and discovered the name of the church at which her husband had served. Mom wrote Lora a note assuring her she would be praying for her, then mailed it to the church in hopes that someone would get it to Lora.

Mom (and my church family) continued to pray for Lora in the days and weeks to come. It was almost seven years later that my mom was curious as to how Lora was doing. On a whim, Mom Googled Lora's name and up popped "Lora Jones' Ministries." Mom followed the link and sure enough—it was our Lora! Mom messaged her and Lora remembered the note of encouragement my mom had sent. My mom shared news of Lora's site with a church friend, who in turn contacted Lora to come and speak at one of our church's women's retreats. It was there that I would have the opportunity to meet Lora again. We hugged and cried together. And from that day forward I have had a relationship with her and am honored to call her "my friend." I am convinced that God put me in Lora's hospital room for a reason—it was no coincidence. I believe I was her nurse because God knew Lora would need a nurse who prayed and believed in a God who doesn't leave us or forsake us."

—Aubrey Gabbard, RN

Part 2

TIMID STEPS OF FAITH

Chapter 3

BLANK PAGES

"The Lord is close to the brokenhearted and saves those who are crushed in spirit."

PSALM 34:18

After the funerals, everyone went back to their own homes, except my precious momma. She stayed with me, so I wouldn't have to be alone. Even with her presence, life became absurdly quiet. The normal sounds of my happy home were silent. I had no idea what to do next. I had no idea how to live life without my soulmate and my children.

I CAN'T

My life's next chapter stared at me with stark white, blank pages. Life left me with nothing to fill the canvas. No ink. No paint. Not even those little blue lines to help write straight. Where once colorful dreams for the future danced, now my mind struggled to form enough everyday sentences to fill an hour, let alone a day.

How can I do this for a lifetime?

In days gone by, I welcomed blank pages. When I completed college—done with tests and papers and homework—I embraced the chance to start anew with "real" life. I loved the feeling of novelty and anticipation each time we moved to a different community and a new church. It gave the opportunity to start over, so to speak, and hopefully change a few things about myself.

This time, however, the blank page felt bleak, meaningless, and overwhelmingly lonely, even surrounded by people who loved me and wanted to ease my pain. No one, nothing, scratched the surface of the ache in my heart.

But thank God, they tried anyway.

No one, nothing, scratched the surface of the ache in my heart.

But thank God, they tried anyway.

Countless people helped me during those days in Miami. One of J.'s closest friends Dale stopped by my house after work every day to see if Mom and I needed anything. Mostly he helped manage the flow of people. I liked to hear from people, and yet it overwhelmed me to respond. Over and over, I found myself repeating, "I don't know," to a host of questions. I didn't know where to live, or where I expected to be for Christmas, or even what I wanted for dinner.

People asked me what they could do for me. I didn't know that either. So they brought food. Lots of it. Somehow most brought Italian food. It became a secret joke Mom and I shared. We ate pasta until we thought we might turn into noodles. At least it brought a crooked smile to my lips when someone brought yet another spaghetti casserole to the door.

Everyone wanted to do and say something helpful. They tried in every way possible to make me feel better. When they couldn't discern what to say, they said nothing at all. They simply wrapped their arms around me and held me. God's comfort came to me through their touch.

I believed the Bible, which says God's future plans for me are still good (Jeremiah 29:11), but it brought absolutely no comfort to me at first. Nothing eased the enormous loss in my heart. One day, a precious older woman, whom I love, quietly sat with me in my living room. She said those dreaded words, "God has something big in mind for you!" Gritting my teeth together, I growled, "He BETTER!" Her eyes grew large and she fell silent. Guilt washed over me. I feared I hurt her feelings, but I meant those bitter words.

When she left, I called Dale. Fearing I would lose my temper with someone who simply tried to bring me comfort, I told him I needed some time without the parade of people at my door. I didn't want to say something I would regret. He put out the word to the church and asked everyone to stop coming for a while. They agreed, and the parade stopped.

It gave me some time to safely lose it, or to simply stare off into space without speaking at all. To begin to absorb the reality of what happened.

Finally, I turned to my mom and said, "I can't do this." My mom amazed me because she didn't try to fix anything. She never did. I do. I attempt to make life better for people—by telling them what to do or trying to change their circumstances. I'm the one who always talks when I should be quiet. She didn't. Instead she held me and listened to me say over and over, "I can't do this."

When she spoke, she simply said, "I know."

We both realized I wasn't strong enough.

It was impossible.

But for God, nothing is impossible.

BACK AND FORTH

A few days later, someone sent me a journal titled, *Comfort in the Mourning* by Connie S. Owens. I don't even remember who sent it, but I am convinced God directed them to do so. A regular blank journal frustrated me at this point, but this one printed a phrase or sentence at the top of each page. When I thumbed through the book, some of those phrases grabbed my attention.

"My precious one has gone on a journey I cannot yet take—how wonderful for them—how lonely for me."[13]

Tears dripped down my face.

That's how I feel, but I didn't know how to say it.

I kept turning the pages and reading.

"The Lord is near to those who have a broken heart. Psalm 34:18."[14]

Yes, Lord, I hear you. Thank you for this gift of blank pages, with some words written by someone who understands.

Each day I looked through that book until I found a phrase which described my feelings, and I responded to it with my shaky pen. It helped me begin to put words to my thoughts and emotions.

Journal Entry: December 21, 2004

"Lost dreams, shattered hopes, an altered future—nothing is as I had planned."[15]

> *Everything is gone. My husband, my daughter, my son, my home, my job, even my calling as a pastor's wife. All future plans are no longer valuable: college funds, retirement, dreams of a home on the lake, traveling the rest of the U. S., our own home again. Nothing matters anymore. There's no one to hand down things to; no one to plan for, no one to create an inheritance, or legacy for. No one to even pass on our name. No grandchildren, no one to care for me when I'm old. All that's left is the dog—and I gave him away—if I can't care for those I long to hold and love, I don't' want to take care of any living thing . . .*

On that same day, I wrote in another entry:

> *When people told me that God must have something great for me to do since He spared me, I thought, "He Better!!" and I said that to several people.*
>
> *But who am I to threaten God? I had to repent to the Lord for that attitude!*
>
> *Now I'm thinking that it would truly be an act of God to simply survive this and go on to a normal, boring life. That would be huge enough. Just to survive. It's not about me. Not my story to write, or change. He doesn't have to explain to me anyway. And explaining wouldn't change a thing.*

Back and forth I swung each day. Yell awhile, trust awhile, yell awhile . . .

CHRISTMAS

As the time came closer to Christmas, a desire grew in me to go to Kansas for the holidays. I couldn't stand the thought of being in the parsonage, with memories of my husband and children everywhere I looked. But one major obstacle stood in the way: due to my concussion, the doctor wouldn't allow me to drive and Mom wasn't willing to drive long distances. So, with a little teamwork, my family formed a relay to get Mom and I from the northeast corner of Oklahoma to my mom's home in the southwest corner of Kansas.

Journal Entry: December 24, 2004

Christmas Eve came without my permission. I tried all day to pretend that it wasn't here. Finally, the tears came anyway. And fear. What will I do and where will I go? It's easier, and feels safer to stay in a fairy tale world—pretending it didn't happen, reading a book and living in that story, daydreaming of past or present or future, just so it's not the real present.

When I am afraid, I will trust in You (Psalm 56:3). Well, Lord, I'm afraid. Help me trust in You. And believe that You are enough.

Lord, please show me where to live and when to move out of the parsonage.

My mind swirls with so many things.

On Christmas Day, my sister-in-law's family invited Mom and I to their home. We ate too much and played cards throughout the afternoon. The day passed better than I imagined possible. I pretended it was an ordinary day instead of Christmas. Since I'd shared our gifts at Thanksgiving, their family graciously waited to exchange gifts until we left, so it proved possible to deceive myself—at least part of the time.

I wish you were here.

That year I had made snowmen Christmas decorations to give as gifts to each of my brothers' families. When I packed the van that fateful day, I included the one I made for myself. At the time, I wondered why I had packed mine. When I discovered some of the snowmen became damaged in the accident, I replaced the pieces of the broken ones with my own and gave everyone a complete set. God amazes me with His details. He knew it mattered to me.

I spent a few days with my Jones family as the calendar turned to a new year. Sometimes there just weren't words to say, so we played cards. It gave us something normal to do together. Slowly, we began to share our thoughts. I asked Jack and Kris several questions about Janessa's experience at the hospital in Wichita, testing to see if my memories matched reality. They did.

My brother-in-law Mark, a police officer in Garden City, gathered my personal belongings from the van after the accident. When he described the condition of the van, he answered a few more of my questions. Now some of my memories made sense. The impact pushed the dashboard into the center of the van. I had leaned back against it when my feet were out the passenger door.

"Were you sitting cross-legged in the seat?" Mark asked me.

"No, my feet were on the floor," I assured him. I sometimes sit with my feet in the chair since I'm vertically challenged, but this time I did not.

"Your legs should have been crushed. There was not room for them between the seat and the dashboard," Mark said.

A thermos at my feet badly bruised one leg, but none of the bones in my legs broke. *They weren't even stuck.*

Why did you protect me? It's so much more reasonable for me to have been killed in the accident too. You left me behind on purpose. Why would you do that?

Why did God leave me behind? I had *no idea*.

I attended church on Sunday, January 2nd, with my Jones family. Memories from the funeral flooded my mind. It seemed unreal. How could it be true? During the worship service, my questions quieted.

Music penetrated my mind and the hymn "Jesus Is All the World to Me,"[16] spoke to my soul. I felt as if I sang *with* Janessa and Jayden.

A few hours later, I wrote in my journal:

"Jesus is all the world to me,
My life, my joy, my all;
He is my strength from day to day,
Without him I would fall:
When I am sad, to Him I go; . . ."[17]

I sang with tears, but I kept singing. As we sang, I thought about the cloud of witnesses we have circling the throne, singing praise to God.[18]

I could hear them cheering me on. "Way to go Mom!" Like they were so excited to hear me praise God with them. Thanks for the encouragement Lord.

ANSWERS

Staying with Mom meant returning to my childhood home. Located ten miles away from the small city of Liberal, her quiet farm sits amidst grassland and wheat fields. Although I have three brothers living here on this earth, and one I never met in heaven, I didn't grow up with them. By the time I reached eight, they were all in college or married. For all practical purposes, I grew up as an only child. I played by myself, creating fun with my imagination.

Our parents had built a miniature house, approximately the size of a tool shed, for my brothers. They made it into a fort or pretended to be cowboys in it. When I got old enough to play outside alone, I renovated it into a miniature kitchen and played house. I loved it out there. I dressed my cats in doll clothes and pushed them around in my baby buggy. In the tall grass under the hedge trees, I made another "house" hidden away in the soft green grass. Laying on my back, I peered up through the leaves to the beautiful blue skies of Kansas.

Far from those blissful days of childhood now, I ached for the peaceful retreat I used to find there. My head swam with questions if I sat and tried to remember—anything. In fact, I couldn't get my memory to work at all. It scared me. I longed to be able to sit in my rocking chair and remember entire stories of Janessa and Jayden—every moment of the fourteen years of motherhood I enjoyed.

I couldn't get my memory to work at all. It scared me.

My mind occasionally short-circuited. Sometimes it seemed like the accident didn't happen, and other times as if my life with J. and the kids didn't occur. I recognized the facts:

J. and I married.

I gave birth to two beautiful children: Janessa and Jayden.

They all died.

Yet, some days, the truth confused me, and I questioned the entirety of it, including my sanity.

So I escaped into books. Mom taught me to be an avid reader. Her shelves overflow with books. We love to read stories, particularly Christian historical fiction. So I pulled a book off the shelf at random. I noticed Mom started to say something but stopped herself. Soon I understood why. The main character of the book survived on the prairies of Kansas, left alone to live following the death of her entire family.

Sigh.

God helped me see possibility through the story. I saw myself through the eyes of the main character. She sat in her rocking chair for hours at a time, until finally, she chose to live. Deep within me, I pondered if I would ever be able to feel enough hope to make the same choice she did. According to the author, it might be possible.

I also spent a lot of time reading the Bible. It might sound rather deep and spiritual, but in truth, I did it simply because J. and I had recently made the commitment to read the same passages each day.

In fact, he had challenged the whole church to read the Bible daily. J. designed a plan with five choices, in order to encourage everyone to try, even if they believed they could only read a few verses at a time. In one year, we could read only the Psalms and Proverbs; the rest of the Old Testament; the gospels; the rest of the

New Testament; or combine the four readings and read the entire Bible. He chose each path, dividing each one into portions to read daily. It took many painstaking hours for him to choose the passages for each day's reading. While I watched him write it, I wondered why he took such time and detail with it since similar ideas already exist. When he finally finished, he made it into a pamphlet.

I'd always wished to read the Bible together with him. It excited me to begin this adventure together. We didn't necessarily read it aloud to each other, but we read the same passages each day, and we discussed what we read. I loved listening to him talk about what the Lord said to him.

It seemed better and easier to start something innovative in January, but urged by God to start sooner, J. obeyed. We began in September. God intended to use his plan specifically for me. He knew me, what loomed around the corner, and what my character lacked. January would be too late. Because J. followed God's instructions, I enjoyed three months of studying the Scripture with my husband.

So I read the Bible for J. My commitment to him helped me stay in the Word, but I must say it shames me to think God knew I wouldn't choose to do it on my own. I'm grateful He recognized my weaknesses and made a way for me ahead of time.

He also planned what I read and when I read it. I really like to picture an angel behind J. while he worked on dividing out the passages. "No, she will need this verse on this day. Move it here." Every time I ponder it, I cry. It's such a tender picture to me—the combination of J.'s love and obedience to God and God's love for me which knit together this reading plan to give me what I needed, exactly when I needed it.

. . . the combination of J.'s love and obedience to God and God's love for me which knit together this reading plan to give me what I needed, exactly when I needed it.

Day after day I read, and God answered my questions through the Scripture. I underlined and dated those verses in my Bible and wrote the references on the inside front cover. God gave me these treasures. From time to time, I reread them, so I always remember what He said at such a tender time in my life. I ran into one of them this morning in my regular Bible reading. Dated January 6, 2005, it fits exactly into the time frame of this chapter. It says:

> *"I will instruct you and teach you in the way you should go; I will counsel you and watch over you. Do not be like the horse or the mule, which have no understanding but must be controlled by bit and bridle or they will not come to you. Many are the woes of the wicked, but the Lord's unfailing love surrounds the man who trusts in him"*
>
> PSALM 32:8-10

I yearned to live this life the way God required. I desired to trust Him. When I questioned how, God made a way for me to begin to understand through the Bible and J.

Journal Entry: December 28, 2004

As shadows of sorrow cover my path, I find myself on a journey of faith.[19]

> *"Now faith is being sure of what we hope for and certain of what we do not see."*[20] *Faith is believing they are in heaven with the Lord and that I, too, will be there one day. That's the easy part. Faith is also believing there's good in my future. That it's OK—whether it is alone or not. That's harder. Faith is patiently listening and waiting for God to speak, not trying to figure it out myself. That's the hardest of all."*

Later, the very same day, He gave me the first steps. I read in I Corinthians 7 during the day. In this chapter, Paul answered some of the questions the Corinthian people asked him. He covered topics like divorce (what to do if your spouse isn't a believer), and remarriage of widows (it baffled me when Paul suggested widows will be happier to remain as they are), and circumcision (the Gentiles didn't need to worry about adhering to that particular Jewish law). Throughout the chapter, three times in fact, Paul says, "Each one should remain in the situation which he was in when God called him."[21] The phrase appeared to be highlighted and in bold to me. It jumped off the page and right into my heart. God whispered, "This is the answer."

Immediately, I grasped two things. First, God led us to Miami to serve at Immanuel Baptist Church. In my journal I wrote, "I am to stay in Miami until He calls me out because I was called there to start with—it wasn't a decision of logic, so neither should leaving be a decision of logic." I should stay in Miami until God said to do something different.

Second, I realized God meant I am still called to ministry. This realization brought me peace and relief. Finally, I'd found something in my life unchanged by the accident: I still wanted to serve God in the ministry, and He still wanted me to do it.

God is acquainted with your situation, and He will answer your questions when you consistently read His words in the Bible. I hope you will take J.'s challenge to read the Bible daily. His Bible Reading Plan can be found on my website. You don't have to wait until September to start.

Chapter 4

A PRAYER FROM HEAVEN

"And the God of all grace, who called you to his eternal glory in Christ, after you have suffered a little while, will himself restore you and make you strong, firm and steadfast."

I PETER 5:10

Time slowed to a crawl when the calendar pages turned to a new year. The ebb and flow of people at Mom's farm was beginning to irritate me, and homesickness flooded my soul. I longed to be nestled in my own home, surrounded by memories. Home beckoned.

CAN I GO HOME?

Journal Entry: January 2, 2005

Others have hurt this badly and lived—I suppose I will also.[22]

> *"Grief is hard work. It leaves me exhausted as I fight to just survive . . . There have been too many people everywhere. I'm finding myself irritable . . . I'm ready to go home and be alone. Yet I know that home really no*

> *longer exists. I hope I find the comfort I'm looking for when I get there."*

My family and I lived in a parsonage for the first time in our ministry career. We owned our own home in both Clay Center, Kansas, and Grand Island, Nebraska, so it seemed strange to move into a house owned by the church in Miami. Over the years, we heard horror stories from other ministry families in parsonages. They told us about church members who dropped by the parsonage for cleaning inspections, and churches which didn't maintain the property.

Our church, however, lovingly prepared the parsonage for us. It looked beautiful. They gave us permission to paint the walls in colors we enjoyed. Janessa helped us paint her room in bright, fun colors. Jayden chose gray to match his theme of black and red. We had fun creating rooms which reflected each of our personalities. In no time, we felt at home. J. and I loved the big backyard and made it perfect by putting in a wonderful pond and stocking it with goldfish. We fully intended to stay at least until the kids graduated from high school.

Now, however, the home was no longer ours. It belonged to the church. When they called another pastor, it would become his home. Although the people of Immanuel agreed to never rush me, I didn't know how long I *should* live there. At some unknown point in the future, I needed to move. I pushed the idea from my mind, unwilling to consider the emotions of walking away from my home. For now, I wanted its comfort.

Can I do it? What will it be like to be alone? Will I crumple into a ball on the floor? Will I scream in pain? Will I sit in silence?

I hoped to go home quietly. If everyone knew when I arrived, I expected to be immediately surrounded by people, ready to help. But I wanted some time by myself to look through everything, and to allow the stories to replay in my memory without anyone observing me. I yearned for the space to mourn—to sob until I could sob no more.

With the help of a couple friends in Miami, and a couple of family members, I decided to go home secretly. The friends prepared my house for my arrival. My nephew and his wife planned to drive me back to Miami and drop me off.

In the meantime, the weather in Liberal turned bad. On the morning we intended to leave, freezing rain fell from a dark sky. The thought of driving on icy roads terrified me. When my nephew chose to wait another day, relief washed over me. With it, came a deep disappointment. I was so ready to be home.

Our weather didn't break until two days later. Finally, I climbed into the backseat of their car and rode in silence. The mixture of fear and anticipation in my heart was palpable. In what seemed like no time at all, we pulled into my driveway. I quietly slipped into my house while my nephew and his wife drove away.

DEAFENING SILENCE

Home. It looked the same. Everything left in its place, like they were simply gone for the evening to a church meeting, or a soccer practice, or shopping with friends. The silence rang in my ears, in a high-pitched hum.

They won't come home. The sounds of their voices will never again sing in the hallways.

As I sank to the floor, I let the tears come until it felt as if my chest collapsed under the weight of the emptiness. Guttural sounds escaped my lips in a desperate attempt to express the pain. My body shook until exhaustion overtook it and allowed deep sleep to come.

The process continued for three days. I didn't go outside at any time. Inside, I walked from room to room trying to memorize everything. Worried I would forget, I took dozens of pictures to help me forever remember every detail with precision.

I always laundered all the clothes before vacations, so when we packed we easily chose anything we wanted. Then, when we returned home, clean clothes hung in the closets. The plan worked well in the past, but now the result of my habit meant nothing smelled like them. Only one of J.'s shirts remained in the laundry basket. I held it, smelled it, and wet it with my tears. Folding it carefully, I tucked it into my dresser drawer, where it stayed for many years, until the "J. smell" completely faded away.

Journal Entry: January 7, 2005

I search for you, but . . . your absence is present everywhere![23]

> *"Well, I've been alone in this house for twenty-four hours. Everywhere I turn the three of you are missing. Nothing is the same in my life except housework and you know how I loved that.*
>
> *Sometimes I talk to you as if you are here, but I try to talk to God instead. I know that I need to throw my energy and love into developing that relationship that the three of you are enjoying to the fullest now.*
>
> *I miss you. I love you. I'm going to be okay. See you soon."*

Journal Entry: January 7, 2005—later that night

> *"Well, I'm home . . . alone. Sometimes I'm overcome by sorrow. I danced with J.'s jean jacket, holding one arm of it behind me, pretending I am leaning on his shoulder. It brought me comfort.*
>
> *Sometimes I'm restless. That's when I watch TV.*
>
> *Sometimes I'm afraid. The only thing for that is prayer.*
>
> *Sometimes I'm at peace. That's the part that is so illogical.*
>
> *I argue with myself. Why am I at peace in the midst of all of this? Am I going crazy? No! Satan is trying to make me think it's crazy to follow God. It's not! God is the one giving me peace."*

LOVE LETTER

I sat down at our computer and found myself reading the last e-mail J. sent before we left on our trip. It went to our good friend, Richard, whose wife faced cancer for the second time. The prognosis gave little hope. When I read the note, I heard J.'s voice in my head. He seemed to be talking to me. Richard's name faded from the page, and I saw my own name instead. I drank in his words:

". . .words cannot begin to express the heaviness of my heart and even if they could, I am not sure where I would begin. I am so sorry that you and [our] family are having to face this struggle, but know that you do not face it alone.

Father, watch over [Lora. She] must have so many questions that [s]he doesn't even know which ones to ask. In addition, [s]he may not want to hear the answers to any of them. Lord, draw [her] close to you and help [her] to see your hand in this. Comfort [her] grieving heart . . . Pour out your strength upon [her] Lord and make [her] strong, firm and steadfast (1 Peter 5:10) . . . Also give [her] the wisdom to know what is important and needs to be taken care of right now and what is not important and can wait. Guide [her] steps and [her] heart during this time.

Again Lord, we ask for full and complete healing, but we do bow to your sovereignty and understand that you know best. Watch over every member of this family and pour out your blessing upon them.

In Jesus' name, we ask these things. Amen

I am praying for you and I love you. Sorry you have to face this difficulty. Looking to Jesus,
JLJ"

As the tears fell down my face, I realized, once again, God brought me the words I needed through J.'s hand. His Bible study plan took me to the Scriptures, but this time, J. prayed for me through his words to Richard. It was a love letter from heaven.

HOMESICK FOR HEAVEN

Following three days home alone, I decided to interact with someone. Since my doctor cleared me to drive after six weeks, I climbed into the pickup and drove to the house of my good friend, Glynda. During the last four years, she and I had spent hours together talking about life and about church. As pastors' wives, we understood each other, and we each sensed a deep calling to the ministry ourselves. Without phoning ahead, I knocked on the door. Her daughter answered. Taken by complete surprise, she became overexcited, shut the door in my face, and ran through the house calling to her mom, "Lora's here!"

While I waited on her doorstep chuckling, I thought about a story in the Bible. King Herod imprisoned Paul for preaching about Christ Jesus. During the night, an angel appeared and let him out of the prison. He went to the home of his friends, interrupting them while they prayed for his release. When the servant opened the door, she closed it in his face and ran to tell the others (Acts 12).

Then the door flew open and my friend enveloped me in her arms. Glynda and I talked and cried together for several hours.

Earlier in the evening, I'd called Dale to let him know I'd left the house. He didn't have to keep my presence a secret anymore. Later, he told me just a few moments after I talked to him, his phone rang, and someone told him my truck had been moved. It still makes me smile to think how closely everyone kept track of me. The entire community of Miami knew I was home within twenty-four hours. They gathered around me, determined to take care of me. I considered myself safe and at home, even though I felt out of place. If home is where the heart is, and three huge pieces of my heart went to heaven, how could I ever feel at home here on earth? MercyMe describes it well in their song, "Homesick."[24]

You're in a better place, I've heard a thousand times
And at least a thousand times I've rejoiced for you
But the reason why I'm broken, the reason why I cry
Is how long must I wait to be with you
I close my eyes and I see your face
If home's where my heart is then I'm out of place
Lord, won't you give me strength to make it through somehow
I've never been more homesick than now.[25]

Chapter 5

THE CHOICE

"My soul is weary with sorrow; strengthen me according to your word."

PSALM 119:28

A house full of stuff. Their precious things. Some valuable because of the memories attached to them. Others worthless, under other circumstances. Faced with thousands of decisions about what to keep and what to take with me when the time came to leave, I realized even the everyday, mundane junk carried meaning for me now. Overwhelmed but determined, I resolved to go through every piece of paper, every folded-up note, every toy. I wanted to remember. Every. Single. Thing.

Journal Entry: January 11, 2005

Mourning is the outward expression of inner pain. I need this time of mourning.[26]

> *"I need this time, but I don't want it. I'm just so very sad. I feel so out of place. I don't want to do any of the things in front of me. I don't know where the drive to go on will come from. I want to push through the process of*

> *going through things so it's over, and yet I do not want to begin because I never want it to be 'over.' Surely it's all still a bad dream and God will fix it somehow. He's always fixed it before."*

An organizer by nature, I wondered how to tackle the huge project in front of me. After days of pondering, I created a strategy. I decided to begin packing, even though I didn't plan to move yet. In my mind, I divided each room into four piles: precious memoirs I intended to display every day, no matter where I lived; beloved possessions I planned to keep, stored in special containers; treasures to be given away to family or friends; and garage-sale-type items. I didn't imagine myself capable of selling anything. Insignificant Kids' Meal toys and Barbie Doll shoes somehow became very valuable to me. It seemed impossible to put a price tag on them. I even struggled to throw away the broken toy pieces. Instead, my plan placed each pile into a box with a detailed label of its contents.

Each piece filled my senses with memories. I heard their voices in my mind while I read the notes, saw their faces in the pictures, touched their soft baby blankets, and smelled J.'s aftershave. Determined to find some way to capture the moments forever, I chose to make notes about the stories and tuck the paper inside the box.

The task looked insurmountable, but I didn't seek any help. People distracted me and might rush me or question my choices. Besides, no one could make these decisions for me. I worked on it a little each day. When I grew weary, I watched television, read a book, or went to visit someone.

Clothes were the easiest place to start. I gave some of J.'s suits to another local pastor, and packed others away to take with me on a mission trip to Brazil planned for the upcoming summer. While thinking about Brazil, I also set aside some of Jayden's Hot Wheels to take to the orphanage.

I normally passed down Jayden's clothes to a young man in our church. Offering them to him again felt completely different this time—so final. No more clothes to buy, no more to share. Furthermore, what if it bothered the boy or his mother to take them this time? I struggled with how to ask in a way which wouldn't be uncomfortable for either one of us. Mom suggested a way to say it which helped make it possible for me.

"It seems my son has outgrown the use of his clothes. Would you like them for your son?" The words refocused me from death to life. Jayden is alive. He simply didn't require earthly clothes anymore.

When I asked the girls in Janessa's youth group if they might enjoy something of hers, they loved the idea. Some of the girls wore the clothes; others made pillows from them. Each of them cherished what they received as a tangible way to remember her.

Pleased to see our friends treasure gifts from our home, I began to think of specific people and ask myself what might be meaningful for them to receive. J.'s books I gave to young men who'd entered the ministry under his mentoring. In this way, J. continued to have a part in their training. It strengthened his legacy in their lives.

Some of their clothing I kept for myself. Even today, their shirts hang in my closet. When loneliness unsettles me, I wear one of those shirts and feel their arms around me once more. It brings the warmth of comfort to my soul.

I also saved a group of T-shirts from each of them. Each one told a story and held a memory. Soccer teams, cheerleading camp, kindergarten class projects, church camps, mission trips, Vacation Bible School, sweatshirts cross-stitched by their Daddy, favorite sayings—shirts which I eventually asked someone to make into a quilt. Those quilts hang over the headboard of my bed today and create a flood of precious memories.

When I finished sorting and distributing clothes and a few treasures to friends, the time came to implement my plan of organizing the rest of their precious belongings. Although I thirsted for the memories the process revealed, it also submerged me in emotional pain, and left me feeling weak and vulnerable.

God's gentle words came to me. "Choose to believe, Lora."

God's gentle words came to me. "Choose to believe, Lora."

A chorus of voices filled my memory.

"This is for my glory."[27]

"I will choose to listen and believe . . ."[28]

"Way to go, Mom! Praise God with us!"

Finally, my own voice joined them, "My heart will choose to say Lord, blessed be your name."[29] The song, "Blessed Be Your Name"[30] by Matthew Redman, continued in my heart:

Every blessing You pour out
I'll turn back to praise
When the darkness closes in, Lord
Still I will say
Blessed be the name of the Lord[31]

It's natural to praise God when "streams of abundance flow,"[32] and "the world's 'all as it should be.'"[33] It's hard to do when, as the lyrics continue, the road is "marked with suffering.[34] To give praise in the desert hurts. God gives blessings, but He also sometimes takes them back. He gave me J., Janessa, and Jayden. Then He took them to heaven with Him.

God didn't leave me empty-handed, though.

God didn't leave me empty-handed, though. He left my heart full of love for my family, my soul filled with the promise of eternal life for the future, and my mind full of memories I can touch when I open the boxes of memoirs. With His promise to be with me in the days ahead, I did not need to be afraid.

I chose to believe and moved forward in the first tiny steps of timid faith.

Chapter 6

JAYDEN'S HEAVEN

". . . and the dead in Christ will rise first."

I THESSALONIANS 4:16

My organizational plan began in Jayden's room. At first glance the space appeared clean. I'd told him to clean up the floor and make his bed before we left on vacation. When I checked, the floor looked good and I'd even complimented him. Now, when I opened his toy closet doors, I discovered where he stuffed everything from his floor. Toys cascaded from the precarious pile onto my feet.

You're an ornery little rascal. Now I get to clean up your mess.

I imagined his impish grin and mischievous eyes twinkling at me. "Aw mom, you just said clean up the floor!" I lifted my face toward heaven and smiled.

JAYDEN'S PIECES

Jayden's room reflected his love for building things. A plethora of construction toy sets filled his closet. He enjoyed it when I helped him clean his room because I helped him find the multitude of tiny pieces he consistently lost. I tried many times to train him to put away the miscellaneous pieces at the end of each day. I even purchased containers, labeled them, and put them in his closet. He put the pieces away when I bugged him about it, but always by the handful into the nearest box. Therefore, the various pieces of Lego sets, Bionicles, Transformers, puzzles, racetracks, miniature skateboard sets with ramps, and BattleBots mingled together in every carefully Mom-labeled box.

My mom and I often worked jigsaw puzzles over the years. I enjoyed the challenge of finding the right piece in the pile of multi-colored shapes. However, this task-at-hand combined numerous and varied puzzles with no pictures to guide me. In the days to come, I spent hours attempting to identify and sort the various pieces into piles in order to build each robot, transformer, or Lego set. What would have been easy for him, proved to be difficult for me. I enjoyed the process, however. Closing my eyes, I imagined his playful voice telling me a story about each one.

As I sat cross-legged in the middle of his floor with numerous piles of pieces surrounding me, I listened to his favorite CDs. Talking aloud to him while I worked, my soul found comfort and cheer when I successfully put together an entire set. When the last piece fit into his favorite Transformer, I found myself shouting, "Look, Jayden! I did it!" Laying onto the carpet, I laughed until I cried.

Most of the time the music formed a peaceful background to the work, but one of the songs particularly caught my attention. The slow, peaceful melody of "Untitled Hymn"[35] by Chris Rice beckoned me to stop and listen.

Weak and wounded sinner
Lost and left to die
O, raise your head for Love is passing by
Come to Jesus
Come to Jesus
Come to Jesus and live[36]

That's how I feel—weak and wounded, lost, and left to die alone.

Now your burden's lifted

And carried far away
And precious blood has washed away the stain . . . so
Sing to Jesus
Sing to Jesus
Sing to Jesus and live[37]

I'm grateful for the gift of forgiveness which came at such great cost to you, but I don't know if I have the heart to sing back to you, not today.

And like a newborn baby
Don't be afraid to crawl
And remember when you walk sometimes we fall . . . so
Fall on Jesus
Fall on Jesus
Fall on Jesus and live[38]

I imagined myself stumbling forward into Jesus' arms. I feel like a newborn baby, unable to do anything except sit on this floor and pretend to play with my son.

Sometimes the way is lonely
And steep and filled with pain
So if your sky is dark and pours the rain . . . then
Cry to Jesus
Cry to Jesus
Cry to Jesus and live[39]

Tears streamed down my face. I cried to Jesus and felt Him wrap His arms around me and draw me close to His chest. "Cry to Me and live," He seemed to whisper into my soul.

My way is incredibly lonely and the depth of my pain unmeasurable. But live? I don't know how to live.

As my tears fell onto Jesus' shoulders, the next verse continued to play:

O, and when the love spills over
And music fills the night
And when you can't contain your joy inside . . . then
Dance for Jesus
Dance for Jesus
Dance for Jesus and live[40]

I pictured the joy-filled faces of Jayden and Janessa while they danced with Jesus. My mind wandered for a moment to Jayden's preschool days. He longed for heaven the way someone advanced in years anticipates the end of life. It scared J. and I the first time we heard him express it. "I want to go to heaven Mom," he said. Fear shot through me, but I held my tongue. J. and I locked eyes, each of us stunned. We never spoke of it.

"I don't want to live on earth anymore."

The older Jayden became, the more he spoke of heaven. By the time he was in middle school, he even added, "I don't want to live on earth anymore." I looked for signs of depression, but his cheerful personality betrayed no such signs. Not knowing what to say or do, I said, "I would miss you, Jayden."

I was right.

After the accident, I shared Jayden's words with Tyson, our youth pastor. "Why did he have such a desire for heaven as a tiny child?" I asked. Tyson paused, considered his words, and told me a story.

It happened a mere six days before the accident. The youth group always met on Wednesday nights for a fun time, complete with supper, games, and Bible study. That night, Tyson overheard a playful argument between Jayden and one of the older youth. Jayden made the matter-of-fact statement, "I'm going to get to heaven first."

"I'm older, so I probably will," the other young man said. "How can we know who will get there first anyway?"

Jayden became adamant. "I will die first," he declared. The older youth chuckled.

Tyson and I sat in silence, overwhelmed by the matching stories. It seemed crazy, but my son appeared to know something unknown to us.

The next time I saw him, I asked the older teen who'd won the argument. He grinned and said, "Jayden did. He insisted he knew. I gave up arguing with him." He paused, watching me with questions in his eyes to which I had no answer.

How did Jayden know he was going to die young?

A few days later, Jayden's Sunday School teacher told me another story. During Bible study class one Sunday morning in early November, Jayden had matter-of-factly told his teacher he didn't think he would live to be an adult. The teacher didn't know what to say or do at the time, nor if he should have told me about it now.

My memories of Jayden's words, the Sunday School teacher's story, and Tyson's story, each confirmed to me how God prepared Jayden for heaven from his beginning. No wonder he longed for it.

Jayden knew, but how did he know? Did you sing to him too? Did you send a message through an angel? Did he dream about it? I wish he could tell me the whole story.

All these pieces of Jayden's life story flitted through my mind as I listened to the song. But when the last verse began to play, the breath sucked out of my lungs.

And with your final heartbeat
Kiss the world goodbye
Then go in peace, and laugh on Glory's side . . . and
Fly to Jesus
Fly to Jesus
Fly to Jesus and live

Fly to Jesus
Fly to Jesus
Fly to Jesus and live[41]

I curled into a ball on the floor and sobbed. It's true. He flew to Jesus, and he lives. Jayden found joy, but my heart cascaded into pieces at my feet.

THE WIDOW AND HER SON

A few days later, I read Luke 7:12-13 in the Bible. It's amazing how the Word of God spoke in new ways when I searched for answers. Passages I'd read many times beforehand took on a completely different meaning this side of the accident.

"As he approached the town gate, a dead person was being carried out—the only son of his mother, and she was a widow. And a large crowd from the town was with her. When the Lord saw her, his heart went out to her and he said, 'Don't cry.'"

Jesus' compassion for the widow overwhelmed my senses. "His heart went out to her." He ached for her. He cared. When someone asks how I'm feeling only to be polite, it is meaningless. However, when someone looks at me with sincere kindness and concern, I feel loved. With an unexpected rush of warmth, God's compassion flooded my soul. It finally dawned on me. His heart goes out to me. I am a widow who buried my only son—and daughter.

Pausing barely a moment to bask in the love, I became perplexed at Jesus' words, "Don't cry,"

Seriously? How? Impossible. Why?

As I scanned through the next verse, I saw Jesus do something amazing. He walked directly to the coffin and touched it (vs. 14). I understood Jewish law prohibited contact with a corpse. Now unclean, He couldn't enter the temple to worship until He cleansed himself.[42]

Why did He risk his own rejection for her?

He cared deeply enough to walk directly into her pain and touch it, quite literally.

No one could have predicted what happened next. Jesus spoke to the dead, "Young man, I say to you, get up!" (vs. 14) Can you imagine the astonished expressions on the faces in the crowd? The traditional noisy mourning ritual came to a stop. Everyone held their collective breath.

Then the miraculous occurred.

"The dead man sat up and began to talk, and Jesus gave him back to his mother" (Luke 7:15).

It makes me smile to envision the tender moment when Jesus returned the son to his mother. I can only imagine what the young man said when he awoke during his own funeral. I bet he kept talking the whole way home, and his mother drank in his every word.

No wonder Jesus said, "Don't cry." He planned to restore her son to life.

The story concludes in the Scripture: "They were all filled with awe and praised God. 'A great prophet has appeared among us,' they said. 'God has come to help his people'" (Luke 7:16).

Jealousy flamed within me.

What about me? Why didn't you raise my son back to life?

God reminded me of another passage of Scripture. I turned to it in my Bible and read the words:

"[13]Brothers, we do not want you to be ignorant about those who fall asleep [this means death], or to grieve like the rest of men, who have no hope. [14]We believe that Jesus died and rose again and so we believe that God will bring with Jesus those who have fallen asleep in him. [15]According to the Lord's own word, we tell you that we who are still alive, who are left till the coming of the Lord, will certainly not precede those who have fallen asleep. [16]For the Lord himself will come down from heaven, with a loud command, with the voice of the archangel and with the trumpet call of God, and the dead in Christ will rise first. [17]After that, we who are still alive and are left will be caught up together with them in the clouds to meet the Lord in the air. And so we will be with the Lord forever. [18]Therefore, encourage each other with these words" (I Thessalonians 4:13-18).

We will find our own little corner of heaven and build something on the floor while he tells me stories.

I imagine it all the time—the moment when Jesus gives my son and daughter back to me. It will happen. He promised.

Jesus is not afraid of our pain. If you invite Him, He will walk into your pain and bring healing. He promised. “The Lord is close to the brokenhearted and saves those who are crushed in spirit” (Psalm 34:18).

You can trust Him too. I hope you will.

Meanwhile, I wonder what Jayden said when he sat up and started talking in heaven. I can’t wait to drink in his words again! We will find our own little corner of heaven and build something on the floor while he tells me stories. Just like old times. Then we will dance with Jesus together . . . and live.

Chapter 7
JANESSA'S STORY

". . . and he healed them."

MATTHEW 4:24

Janessa loved to sing. In my mind's eye, I see her seated on the steps of the platform at church with a microphone in her small three-year-old hand. I sat beside her to give her courage. Her uncertainty came from looking at the people, not from singing for them. In typical grade school insecurity, she stopped church performances for a while, but she didn't stop making music. With friends or family, we belted out melodies to the radio while riding in the van, plunked out a tune on the piano at home, or hummed whatever song came to mind when the urge hit us. Her daddy continually changed the lyrics to existing songs just to make her laugh. Melody filled our everyday lives.

JANESSA'S SONG

Our youth group attended two camps each summer. The first one, with about five hundred in attendance, encouraged the students to audition for their talent show. On her second year of camp, Janessa felt brave enough to perform for the judging team. When they chose her to sing for the whole camp, her spirit soared.

Her youth pastor ran the sound booth and recorded her performance, so I got to view it later. During her performance, the microphone died. She talked with her eyes to the ones running the system. When she followed their suggestions, and tried wiggling the cord, her eyes danced. Never missing a beat of the melody or the words, her confidence shined. At the last chorus, the sound came back on and she concluded with a smile and the characteristic shrug of her shoulders. The audience erupted in applause. My Momma-heart swelled with pride.

The second camp came later in the summer. A much larger group, approximately 6,500 kids, gathered to worship and learn about the Lord together. J. attended as a sponsor, and both of our children were campers. When I visited the camp during the week, I loved worshipping with them. I sensed the presence of God among us. The music filled my soul with encouragement. Afterward, I learned Janessa came to a monumental decision in her life earlier in the week. She wanted to sing professionally for her Lord. Again, pride filled me from head to toe. The future seemed bright.

When we returned home, she wondered what to do next to prepare herself for a future in the music industry. She prayed about it at length but became frustrated when she didn't hear any direction from God about her career. She talked with her youth pastor about it and he encouraged her to simply wait for the next step. He assured her God would make the steps clear in time.

Two months later, God took Janessa to heaven.

When I was sorting her things, I found that camp recording and slid it into the DVD player. I watched Janessa sing for camp again. Stunned by the words she sang, I found myself asking the same questions she did six months ago. What do I do next? Am I courageous enough to make the same choice she did?

The pathway is broken
And the signs are unclear
And I don't know the reason why You brought me here
But just because You love me the way that You do
I'm gonna walk through the valley

If You want me to

'Cause I'm not who I was
When I took my first step
And I'm clinging to the promise You're not through with me yet
So if all of these trials bring me closer to You
Then I will go through the fire
If you want me to

It may not be the way I would have chosen
When you lead me through a world that's not my home
But you never said it would be easy
You only said I'll never go alone

So when the whole world turns against me
And I'm all by myself
And I can't hear You answer my cries for help
I'll remember the suffering Your love put You through
And I will go through the valley
If You want me to.[43]

Janessa did everything God asked her to do. She answered His calling with faith, following Jesus through a world which wasn't her home. I am confident she did not walk alone from this world to the next one. Jesus held her hand during every step.

. . . she did not walk alone from this world to the next one. Jesus held her hand during every step.

Now, it's my turn to sing the song. "It may not be the way I would have chosen,"[44] but I don't walk this life alone either. With my daughter, I choose to say, "I will go through the valley, if You want me to."[45]

JANESSA'S WORDS

Organizing Janessa's room differed immensely from sorting the game pieces of my son. A few favorite stuffed animals lazed on a shelf, but otherwise, the room displayed no toys. Instead, the room reflected what she loved: friends, music, and books.

Books filled the headboard of her bed. *She Said Yes: The Unlikely Martyrdom of Cassie Burnall* laid open and facedown to hold her place in the story of the 1999 shooting at Columbine High School. Her Bible rested beside it, with Bible study books and notebooks full of notes. On top of the headboard, her fancy CD tower sparkled with blue lights when the water feature in the center bubbled. The bookcase held treasure chests of gifts from her friends, and her puppy Beanie Baby collection from childhood. Her dresser displayed pictures of her and her friends laughing and sharing life together.

Janessa loved to write and excelled at it. I read everything I found that she wrote, including her journals and her Bible study books. Even though it probably would have mortified her, I heard her voice in the written pages and soaked in her every word. Sometimes I still tease her friends about seeing their notes to each other. Worry flashes across their faces for a moment, followed by a gentle blush and ornery grin. It makes me smile. Truthfully, I took most of their little folded notes and put them in a box, leaving the personal notes between friends unread.

On her dresser, however, I found a small piece of paper folded in triangles like junior high girls do, with a name on the outside. It appeared ready to go to one of her friends, but it hadn't been delivered yet.

I opened it. Inside it read:

> *"Read carefully!*
> *Hey, what up?*
> *Well, for starters I wanna tell ya that I'm a Christian. OK. Got that? Now I wanna tell ya a story. This is how it goes . . .*
>
> *Once there was this little girl, about 10, who was at the house of a family that went to her church. It was Thanksgiving and she was just enjoying all the many desserts that little girls eat on Thanksgiving. Little did she know what was in store for her the next day.*

That very night, the girl went to fall sleep in her parent's bed. This had become a regular thing: at her bedtime the girl would fall asleep in her parent's bed. When they finally decided to go to bed, they would just move their sleeping little girl to her own, soft bed. But on this particular night, while her parents were downstairs, her mother heard Jesus telling her to go tuck her baby girl in NOW. So, she did. Just as she entered the room she saw her daughter lying there, [making bubbling sounds. When she sat down beside her, all sounds stopped.] Her mother immediately screamed for her husband and went to call 911. The paramedics arrived and soon after that the little girl was taken to the hospital. The girl stayed in the hospital that night and went home the next day. [After some tests, they discovered that the girl was having seizures.] Later, while she was taking a nap she had another seizure. She was taken back to the hospital, stayed there for a while and was given some medicine to help with her seizures.

. . . I am healed and I am able to run and swim and climb a tree . . .

A few weeks after she had her seizures she was looking through her Bible and found this scripture:

'News about him (him is Jesus) spread all over Syria & people brought to him all who were ill with various diseases, those suffering severe pain, the demon-possessed, those having seizures, and the paralyzed and he healed them.' Which is found in the book of Matthew, Chapter 4 & Verse 24.

Now, this little girl had grown up in a Christian home where Jesus was often taught and talked about. When she was about 4 or 5, she decided that she needed to listen to Jesus [herself] and she decided to do what is called accepting Jesus as her Savior. That's a fancy way of saying that she asked Jesus to forgive her for all the bad things she had done and that she was sorry and that she wanted Jesus to become a daily part of her life. Since she was a Christian when she read this verse in the Bible, she knew that Jesus was telling her something. What she thought he was telling her was just what the verse in the Bible said: [Jesus could heal people with seizures.]

Her parents had watched her fall asleep every night since her seizures. Just in case. They were still terrified. But the girl remained calm at all times and patiently told her parents over and over again that she wouldn't have any more seizures. 'How can you be so sure?' they would ask. And she would reply, 'I don't know. I just am.' Because she truly had not recognized the promise that Jesus had made to her when she highlighted that verse in the Bible. She didn't recognize it for a long time until one day her mom borrowed her Bible and found that verse highlighted. As the girl and her mom talked, she finally understood that Jesus had promised He would heal her when she read that verse.

. . . I wanna tell you something. That little girl was me. The only reason I'm alive today is because of Jesus. He spoke to the Christians in my church and told them to pray for me. They did. It seems like everyone I knew then was praying for me. Jesus heard those prayers and now, all thanks and praise to Jesus, I am healed and I am able to run and swim and climb a tree—which are things that I wouldn't have been able to do much of w/ out being healed. I hope that this story of what Jesus is to me changed your life as much as it did mine.

Thanks for listening.

I love U,

Janessa

P. S. Please w/b w/your response to me soon!"

My eyes flooded with tears.

I'm so proud of you, Baby Girl. And I'm thrilled to have your faith story written in your own words.

It humbled me to know her belief in God grew because of the seizures, when mine struggled. I remembered the emotions of dealing with the seizures. Janessa challenged my faith to believe God healed her. I spent most of those days terrified of losing her. Her seizures came at night. Every morning I feared finding her dead. How ironic today.

"The only reason I'm alive today is because of Jesus."

The last section of the note amazed me. *"The only reason I'm alive today is because of Jesus."* I needed those words. They reminded me of the truth: Janessa is alive.

Janessa boldly challenged her Christian friends to live out their faith, but it took more courage to talk to someone who might not be enthusiastic about her faith. I wondered how long it laid on her dresser, whether she wrote it the week of the accident or if she wrestled with delivering it for a while—and I even wondered if I should deliver it to her friend.

What do you want me to do with it, Sweetheart?

Even as I asked the question, I knew what she expected me to do. The note said it all. I delivered the note to her friend and explained what Jesus did for Janessa, which gave her eternal life. Not only did God save her life by rescuing her from the seizures as a young girl, but God saved her life by providing a way for her to enter heaven. God's Son, Jesus, paid the penalty of sin on our behalf, enabling us to be in God's presence. Janessa is very much alive today because of Jesus. I'm confident she runs and swims and climbs trees in heaven right now while singing at the top of her lungs. She sings professionally for her Lord, full-time, face-to-face. I can't wait to be in that concert hall.

Jesus will forgive you and me too, and give us eternal life. If she could, Janessa would write you a note all about it. Maybe she did.

Chapter 8

REMEMBERING THE PAST

"Sustain me according to your promise, and I will live; do not let my hopes be dashed."

PSALM 119:116

People tease me because I'm short. When I started school, my brother told me to take a step stool with me to the bus, in case I couldn't reach the first step. I refused, but the stretch challenged my little legs. My first grade teacher humiliated me when she made me use a kindergarten chair, but it did keep my legs from dangling. Even as an adult, my toes didn't reach the floor in my mom's kitchen table chairs.

UNEXPECTED CONFIDENCE

Always looking up to people, I identify not only with Zacchaeus, the wee-little man who climbed a tree to see Jesus, but also with David, the young man who faced a nine-foot giant. The story of David's unexpected confidence encourages me.

The youngest of eight brothers, David was the designated sheepherder. He spent most of his time out in the fields tending the sheep. One day, his father called him out of the pasture. When he hurried in, he found Samuel the famous prophet in the family tent. I can imagine David's astonishment when Samuel said to David's father Jesse, "Yes, this is the one."

Samuel approached David with a flask of oil. While he spoke, he poured the oil on David's head, anointing him to be the next king.[46]

Overwhelming doesn't even touch the implication of this announcement. Can you imagine the shock? I wonder if an older brother grumbled it should have been him instead. David's face probably reflected complete bewilderment. His father's chest puffed out and he grew an inch with pride. Maybe his mother began planning the coronation party in her mind, or maybe she filled with fear for his safety from the present king.

King Saul, Israel's reigning king, failed to lead the people to serve God. God told Samuel He planned to intervene in the situation and asked him to anoint the next king. Only God knew when the exchange would occur.

While David waited for Samuel's prophecy concerning his kingship to come true, he continued taking care of the sheep. He played the harp in the pasture, both to soothe the animals and to lift his voice in praise. Through his songs and poems, David talked with God about the situation. Sometimes he rested near the babbling brook in the quiet meadow. Other times, he cried out to God when predators attacked the flock.

David found extraordinary strength to defeat lions and bears when he prayed.[47]

During this time, the people of Israel battled against the Philistines. David's oldest three brothers joined the troops. Once again, Jesse called David home from the pasture. This time, he asked David to check on his brothers at the battle line.

When David arrived, he discovered the Israelite army on one hill, and the Philistines on another. In the valley between them stood the Philistine's mightiest warrior, Goliath. The sound of the giant's voice echoed across the hills. ". . . Choose a man and have him come down to me. [9]If he is able to fight and kill me, we will become your subjects; but if I overcome him and kill him, you will become our subjects and serve us" (I Samuel 17:8b-9).

Goliath's challenge struck fear into the hearts of the Israelite warriors. Nine feet tall, with a plumed helmet on his head, making him appear even taller, he seemed unstoppable. They felt like grasshoppers in comparison.

To make matters worse, according to I Samuel 13:19-22, solely King Saul and his son Jonathan carried weapons. The rest of the army relied on sticks, clubs, or their bare hands. The huge javelin in Goliath's grip dwarfed Israel's best swords. The Bible says in I Samuel 17:7, the head of his spear weighed more than 15 pounds. Imagine the weight of a small child sitting on the end of your spear.

Goliath smiled with confidence. The Israelites shook in fear.

Who had the courage to fight a giant? No one. Not even the king himself, who stood a head taller than everyone else.[48] If *he* refused to go out and fight against Goliath, no one else dared.

Terror and hopelessness engulfed the troops. They waited for the inevitable.

Slavery. The word tasted bitter on their lips.

The giant began to mock the name of God. David grew indignant. He ignored the fear of the Israelites and sprang to action. He believed in the power of God to move in impossible situations. The strength of God surged within him when he rescued a sheep from a lion's mouth—this would be no different. He recognized his God could win this battle! So, he volunteered to fight Goliath.

Doubtful but desperate, the king agreed. He offered his armor to David, but it swallowed his small stature.

So David faced Goliath with merely his slingshot, unexpectedly confident, based on his faith in his powerful God.

The warriors held their breath. Their lives rested in his small hands.

He chose a stone, put it in the leather pouch, and flung it through the air with the precision of an expert.

Zing.

It hit the enemy between the eyes.

The air split with the cheer from the Israelite army when Goliath crashed to the ground. Running quickly to him, David grabbed Goliath's own sword and cut off the giant's head.

A small one with mighty faith saved the day.[49]

BEARS AND LIONS

David approached the giant with confidence because he knew God by experience. His previous victories over bears and lions convinced him of God's power. I doubt when he killed the lion, he thought, "Now I'll be able to kill a giant." No, instead, his knowledge gave him increasing assurance to rely on God, whatever the situation. Therefore, when he met the giant, he stood fearless.

These impossible situations dare us to rely on God's power to prevail.

"Bears and Lions" teach us faith in God. These impossible situations dare us to rely on God's power to prevail.

Janessa's seizures were my "bears and lions." I didn't know at the time what they prepared me to face, but now I do.

One night, a few days before Thanksgiving, I sent nine-year-old Janessa and six-year-old Jayden upstairs to bed, and promised to come tuck them in. I stayed downstairs for a while, working on Christmas presents. Distracted with the gifts, time passed quickly, and the kids fell asleep without me. When I realized it, I sensed an urge in my spirit to put down my work and go upstairs to check on them anyway.

I opened the door to our bedroom, where Janessa fell asleep. Strange noises began coming from her throat. Perplexed, I sat down beside her on the bed. Then the noises stopped, and she appeared to completely quit breathing. I screamed for J. and he bounded up the stairs. He carried her into the kitchen near the phone. We called 911 and waited. With my heart pounding in my ears, I knelt beside her with tears streaming down my cheeks. Looking at her small face, I said to God, "I know she's yours, but can we keep her a little while longer?"

I'll always believe God answered my prayer in that moment.

"She has a seizure disorder," the doctor told us. "Expect them to come mostly at night." They gave us a medication to help, but terror reigned in my life each time Janessa climbed in bed. We set a baby monitor in her room, but often, we simply slept on the floor beside her bed.

I wrestled to learn to trust God with my daughter, and to not let fear completely consume my soul. Over the next few months, the medication appeared to stop the seizure activity. I began to slowly relax.

By the time Janessa turned ten, we moved from Nebraska to Oklahoma. When we found a new pediatric neurologist, he continued the same treatment at our request. The following year, he suggested we take Janessa off the medication and see if the seizures returned. Appalled and terrified, I discouraged the idea. Janessa, on the other hand, wanted to try it. She acted optimistic and confident—a child's naiveté, I thought. But when J. sided with Janessa and the doctor, they outnumbered me. The medication stopped.

I began to wait for the inevitable.

Seizures.

The word tasted bitter to my tongue.

HEALING PROMISE

One day, a few weeks later, I picked up Janessa's Bible instead of my own. When I found the passage I sought, I noticed an underlined verse on the same page. In my own Bible, when a verse particularly speaks to me, I underline it and date it, so I'll always remember. Janessa apparently copied my method. In the margin, she had written June 8, 2001. Intrigued, I read the verse. "News about him spread all over Syria, and people brought to him all who were ill with various diseases, those suffering severe pain, the demon-possessed, those having seizures, and the paralyzed, and he healed them" (Matthew 4:24).

Jesus healed seizures. I wonder why I never noticed this word in the Bible before.

I called my daughter to me and asked her what it meant to her. In her childlike way, she told me, "The verse says He heals seizures." In her mind, if He can, He did. She believed God healed her.

"Is that why you weren't afraid to stop the medicine?" I asked. She smiled, characteristically shrugged, and said she guessed so.

"Then why am I afraid, when the God of the Universe said you are going to be okay?" She lifted her shoulders again as if to say, "I dunno," and ran off to play. I sat there dumbfounded.

The date in her Bible preceded our decision to cease medication by approximately nine months. Her confidence wasn't childhood optimism at all, it was childlike faith. Her faithful God did not disappoint her. The seizures never returned. This story gave her unexpected courage. It became the way she told her friends about God—the note I found on the dresser was a prime example.

. . . He gifted me with five extra years with my daughter and the seeds of faith I needed to face her death.

God taught me to trust Him through my children. The healing stories of the scriptures became real. I've read the miracles of Jesus many times, but for Him to intervene and heal my own daughter—amazement and awe overcame me.

I didn't know until much later how much He really gave me the day I asked for more time with my daughter. In the quietness of the days following her funeral, God reminded me of my request. Overwhelmed with the love of my Father, I realized He gifted me with five extra years with my daughter and the seeds of faith I needed to face her death.

What happened to David? For several difficult years, King Saul tried to kill David and prevent him from becoming the next king.[50] Sometimes David felt forgotten by God, but he always returned to the faith he gained through facing the giant. In due time, God kept His promise, and David became King, just like Samuel had said.[51]

Sometimes I feel forgotten too, especially when I am lonely or afraid. Life can be difficult and frustrating. Those days, I try to remember the "lions and bears"—those times when God intervened in my world and displayed his amazing power. When I recall those stories, it renews my faith, hope, and courage.

My dear friends, when you struggle to have faith, call out to God like David did in Psalm 119:116, "Sustain me according to your promise, and I will live; do not let my hopes be dashed." And remember your own stories of God's power.

Remember.

God kept His promise to David.

God kept His promise to Janessa.

God kept His promise to me.

Janessa and David stand in the presence of the King of Kings. God kept His promise of salvation *and* resurrection for *both* David *and* Janessa. I can imagine their lively conversations in heaven about the power their Father God displayed during their lifetimes.

My story is still being written, but God will be faithful to keep His promises to me in the future. I believe Him and trust Him.

He will keep His promises to you too. God is faithful. Please trust Him with me. He will not forget us. Together, let's choose to remember the "bears and lions," even when God seems quiet for a while. Remembering will bring unexpected confidence. Forgetting will bring bitterness to your lips.

Chapter 9

J. L.'S DREAM

"By this all men will know that you are my disciples, if you love one another."

JOHN 13:35

During the summer of 2004, J. received an unexpected phone call from the City Inspector. He wanted a knowledgeable group of volunteers to repair a home for an older man. The story piqued J.'s interest.

THE HOUSE LOVE BUILT

Mr. Woods had lived in this house for most of his life. After a short stint in the military, he returned to live with his mother. They lived together for many years, taking care of each other, until she recently passed away. At 82, Mr. Woods wanted to live out the rest of his days in his childhood home. However, it required significant repair in order to be safe for him.

Interested, J. called Dale, and they drove to the project site. While they walked around the house, listing the repairs, J.'s excitement grew. Not afraid of hard work, he loved to tackle something innovative. In college, he'd studied to be an engineer. Even though his calling led him away from the career, he still loved to take things apart and make them work again. His meticulous mind easily developed a working plan for this adventure. He might not identify every detail, but he wasn't afraid to ask questions or to try new things. Undaunted by the hole in the roof and the collapse in the flooring, the two friends charged forward with enthusiasm to help our comrade, Mr. Woods.

Although we believed God would provide for the unknown, Adult Protective Services required us to lay out the entire plan ahead of time. Our small congregation had to prove our financial backing, find enough volunteers, secure contributors for the materials, and hire a contractor to oversee the work. Step-by-step, God led the way. J.'s excitement spread, and by fall, the goal appeared in sight.

November came, and our anticipation built to an all-time high. By the end of the month, the team completed the planning and paperwork, and waited for final approval and the meeting to sign the contracts.

On the weekend before Thanksgiving, J. received approval of the paperwork. With the verbal approval, they gave him permission to knock down one of the outbuildings ahead of signing the contracts. J. was barely able to contain his excitement. He dropped everything and called Dale. They met at the building site.

They say the only difference between boys and men is the size of their toys. It's the truth.

J. jumped into the Bobcat (skid-steer), smiling ear to ear. He knocked down the first old wall with ease. Scooping up the debris with his equipment, he lifted the bucketful of concrete high into the air and headed toward the dumpster. In his excitement, he didn't consider the uneven ground. He bounced straight into a hole. Slowly, the whole thing tipped over on its nose. When the dust settled, Dale saw J. sitting in the seat, his eyes as big as saucers, looking straight at the ground. Undaunted, he pondered a moment, then lowered the bucket which caused the Bobcat to sit upright again. Pleased with himself, he glanced around to see his friend's reaction to his blunder. Dale shouted at him, "Stick to preachin', Preacher!" Lively laughter from both men rang in the crisp air, loud enough to be heard by the neighborhood.

It's hard to describe the laughter Dale and J. often shared. They slapped each other's shoulders, threw back their heads and laughed until a few tears shone in their eyes. Best friends bring laughter, without a doubt.

It makes me happy to hear Dale laugh. If I close my eyes and listen with my heart, I can hear J. laughing with him again.

The organization scheduled the meeting to sign the contracts on the Tuesday evening before Thanksgiving, November 23, 2004. Since our family planned to leave for our holiday trip as soon as school released, J. called his team and encouraged them to go ahead with the meeting.

"You can do it without me," he said.

Prophetic words.

"You can do it without me," he said.

Prophetic words.

The team signed the agreement at 7:00 p.m. and the accident occurred about 9:30 p.m. Truly, the church built this house without him physically, but their love for him gave them the energy to do it. The newspaper headline read, "The House That Love Built."

Our contractor intended to rebuild about half of the house, leaving part of the original house intact. However, when the first wall came down, exposing the stem walls of the foundation, safety demanded otherwise. The entire house needed to be rebuilt.

Mr. Woods faced the change with difficulty, but he bravely embraced it. We built a small home on his land and furnished it with simple furniture to accompany his own salvageable belongings. I gave him Jayden's bed to sleep in, so he didn't have to sleep on the floor anymore.

Journal Entry: May 5, 2005

"J.,

This morning dawned warm and bright. It was a beautiful day for the open house. I wish you were here to see what we accomplished! You would be so proud of your church family! We pulled together, and with the help of the community, built an entire house! You should have seen the smile across Mr. Woods' face while

he showed off his new house to all the people who came. His family came, some even from as far as California. He and his brother played the guitar and harmonica for us at the celebration. Of course I cried, but it was amazing to be able to fulfill your dream. Your Mom and Dad came, and your sister Jana. Everyone is so proud of you, and all you accomplished.
I miss you."

The dedication of the home celebrated the lives of two men: Rev. J. L. Jones and Mr. Earl Woods. J. envisioned our church faithfully following God in his work. Mr. Woods hoped to live on his own land for the rest of his life. The home fulfilled both dreams.

Twelve years later, Mr. Woods still lives in the same small house.

Why did we build a home for a man we didn't know, who didn't attend our church, or any church, for that matter? Because the love of God flowed through us to Mr. Woods. God loves him even more than the church family who built his house.

J. often said in his sermons, "Let the Church be the Church!" Those words come from an old hymn, "The Church Triumphant."[52] When J. quoted it, he meant our church should do what God intended every church to do—to reflect God's character to the world.

Let the Church be the Church,
Let the people rejoice.
For we've settled the question,
We've made our choice.
Let the anthems ring out,
Songs of victory swell
For the church triumphant is alive and well.[53]

God works through those who choose to believe in Him. Every time we display God's love to the world, we prove His existence to others, so they can trust Him too. When Immanuel Baptist Church chose to build Mr. Woods' house, I think everyone in heaven rejoiced in victory, their pastor included.

Part 3

THE DAWN OF HOPE

Chapter 10

A WAY THROUGH THE DARKNESS

". . . Daughter, your faith has healed you. Go in peace."

LUKE 8:48

Journal Entry: February 17, 2005

Some days I wonder how I could have come so far and still have so far to go.[54]

> *"Boy, this is how I feel. Most of the legal matters are done, most of the thank you notes are written, most of the initial financial decisions are over. But, oh my, what is next is way overwhelming. I don't want to walk it. There's a lot of deep pain just ahead. I long, with everything I have, to go around it, but I know I can't. The only way to cope is through it. I have started the journey through it—crying until I think my heart could literally break into pieces. And I have found comfort in the Lord there. Maybe I shouldn't fear. After all, He clearly said DO NOT BE AFRAID."*

Somebody once told me, "The shortest distance through anything is straight through the middle of it." If I applied the advice to the painful journey of grief, perhaps the trip could be shortened. The powerful agony overwhelmed me. Desperate to find some way to ease its intensity, I hoped to condense the process and find hope by running quickly through the darkness. Otherwise, I might fall apart.

. . . I hoped to condense the process and find hope by running quickly through the darkness.

PAINFUL JOURNEY

I thought pastor's wives lived in glass bubbles. Everyone watched everything I did—how I reacted to my husband, how I raised my kids, whether I lived what I taught from the Scriptures. Since I perceived my actions affected my husband's ministry, I tried to hide where I failed. With no safe place to fail, or at least admit my failures without expecting condemnation, I became increasingly lonely throughout the years we served in churches.

I'm no longer a pastor's wife, but people seem to be watching even more closely now—and there are more of them! Am I free to let people see my failures now? Or should I continue to keep my wrestling and failures hidden?

To make matters worse, people often said, "J. and the kids are watching you—looking down on you." They meant to comfort me, but honestly, it added to my growing panic.

J., Janessa, and Jayden observe everything I do?!? What if I talk more about Jayden today, will that make Janessa sad? Do they see me when I lose my temper and beat my pillow at night? If they are watching from heaven, I can't go into the other room until I get myself under control. There's no place to hide!

One day, God led me to a song which helped me gain a new perspective. "Unaware"[55] by MercyMe describes someone's reaction when they arrive in heaven and finally talk to God.

"Forgive me if I stare, but I am taken back, that you would let me here, regardless of my past. Oh my hands are

shaking now, but I catch my breath somehow. Oh, I am free at last!
Unaware of my fears, unaware of my shame. Nothing else matters here, but glorifying Your name. Unaware of everything, knowing You're aware of me.
Tell me how I got here, I couldn't make it on my own. Just tell me I can stay, cause it feels so much like home. And I lose all track of time, when I look into your eyes. Your love is all I know.
I'm aware I'm in a place I couldn't be, if you weren't there to call my name and rescue me.
Unaware of my fears, unaware of my shame. Nothing else matters here, but glorifying Your name . . . Unaware of everything, knowing You're aware of me."[56]

Finally, it dawned on me. Heaven contains the majesty of God. Enthralled by His powerful essence, they now understand the overarching plan for our existence. My mundane struggles and victories, pale in comparison to their perspective of the cosmos. I don't have to be afraid of them watching my every move or learning my secrets. Their eyes focus on Someone of significantly greater importance.

This realization, however, didn't change the situation on earth. Even at Wal-Mart or the grocery store, I sensed the eyes of people observing me.

A new idea occurred to me.

Possibly they didn't know how to survive hurt either. Perhaps if I displayed my pain in public, honestly, without hiding my failures, then maybe, just maybe, they would share too, and I wouldn't feel so alone.

HELP FOR THE PAIN

The agony of loss is difficult to describe. It's more than emotional hurt; it's physical too. Sometimes my heart experienced such pressure and stabbing sensations, I expected it to literally break in two. Other times, I wondered if I could tear it open with my own fingers in utter anguish. Instead of getting easier, the ache drove deeper and deeper as time moved forward. At first, shock prevented me from feeling. When the numbness wore off, the torment became excruciating: physically, mentally, and emotionally. Exactly like He said, God's hand shielded me from the weight of the pain in those early days when I felt covered by a blanket from heaven.

When the numbness wore off, the torment became excruciating: physically, mentally, and emotionally.

Sometimes the heartache expressed itself in tears and sometimes in shaking. The shaking came from deep within me, occasionally visible to others, and often not, but either way, uncontrollable. Every muscle in my body tightened. Crying helped release those muscles, but the crying itself created its own misery. An elephant sat on my chest and made it difficult to breathe.

I hate to weep, but it became unavoidable. It released the built-up pressure inside of me. When it came over me, I tried desperately to stop the episode before the uncontrollable shaking and sobbing began. Often unable to do so, I succumbed to the emotions which raged through my body. When the storm finally subsided, I dropped in a heap like a rag doll thrown on the floor and fell into a deep sleep, utterly exhausted.

It exasperated me when it happened in public.

One episode came during children's night at an evangelistic event. The minister read a book called, *Love You Forever*[57] to the audience. With powerful imagery, the book tells of a mother's relationship with her son. Throughout the book, the baby boy keeps growing older, but the mother's words remain the same. "I'll love you forever, I'll like you for always, as long as I'm living my baby you'll be."[58] (I won't spoil the ending, but it's a meaningful read for any age.)

Since the book held tender memories for me, I struggled for control of my emotions while the minister read the pages. I considered leaving the church service, but I didn't want to draw attention to myself. Bit by bit, my silent tears threatened to take control. When I rose from my seat to leave, several friends followed me out of the sanctuary. I collapsed in a chair in a classroom and completely lost control, sobs racking my body. They gathered around me, taking turns praying, singing, or quoting scripture until the storm subsided. Their love overshadowed my embarrassment.

It's ridiculous to struggle with asking for assistance when I know people are willing to help. I guess I want to be self-sufficient. Perhaps it's simply pride in my way. I needed people to notice and act anyway—because my stubbornness refused to cry out, "Help me."

I wish I learned this lesson for the last time, but it's still difficult to say, "I need help."

QUESTIONS

Almost everywhere I went, people hugged me and said something akin to: "I know you aren't supposed to question God, but . . ." I saw the questions in their eyes, and understood them, even though they usually stopped without asking.

Why did this happen? How could God let *this happen? If it could happen to you, and you were following God in the ministry, then what's going to happen to my family? Is this what it costs to follow God? What does it cost to* not *follow Him?*

I pondered these and a host of other questions. I concluded we *can* ask God about them. After all, God is our perfectly kind Father in heaven. Doesn't a good dad encourage his kids to talk with him about the things which confuse them? I let my kids ask *me* questions. In fact, we even encouraged questions with the age old saying, "The only dumb question is the one not asked."

Why not ask? Maybe He will answer.

Thousands of questions rattled through my mind. I believed only one Person can answer those questions. So, I asked them. God didn't chastise me for asking. And sometimes—sometimes—I heard an answer.

Journal Entry: February 19, 2005

God sees my tears as unspoken words from the depths of a wounded heart.[59]

> *"As I read in II Kings today about the Shunammite woman's son being brought back to life, I questioned*

> *God again. 'Why couldn't you have done that for me? Why couldn't you have left me one child?' He answered, 'Do you want them to leave me?'*
> *No, no, I don't. I wouldn't do that to them. I wept. I imagined myself cradled on His lap.*
> *I prayed for memories this morning. I know the only way to them is through the pain. It just hurts so badly. The valley is so long. I don't know if I can do it."*

He didn't directly answer my question, but He did respond to me. It helped me change my perspective from my own suffering to their joy. I wanted, and assumed I needed, a lot more answers, but this gave me a good place to start.

SOPHISTICATED DEFENSE

Twice in my life, traumatic experiences led to clinical depression. Following the accident, it appeared completely reasonable for me to seek psychological help for the illness again. But I didn't.

Why?

That question I *can* answer.

God's healing power.

When we moved to Miami in 2000, I suffered with severe depression. It took its toll on both J. and I, and on our marriage. Following the move, I avoided big projects and difficult tasks. Instead, I concentrated on rest. It took a lot of energy to make basic decisions.

I didn't expect God's direct intervention.

Following the song service one Sunday morning, I settled into my seat in the choir loft. J. walked to his place behind the pulpit, his back facing me. He read from the Bible about a miracle of healing from Jesus' life here on earth. In the story, Jesus walked through a mass of bustling people. He suddenly stopped and asked who touched him. Peter said, "Master, the people are crowding and pressing against you."[60]

Maybe dozens of people brushed by, but Jesus knew one reached out on purpose. He said, "Someone touched me; I know that power has gone out from me."[61]

A trembling woman made her way through the crowd and fell at his feet. She didn't wish to bother Him nor bring attention to herself, but she hoped for healing. So, when Jesus came by, she intended to discretely touch the edge of his robe. *It will be enough,* she thought. The moment she touched Him in faith, He healed her.

As J. continued his sermon, God surprised me by speaking to *me.* "Why have you not asked me to heal you?"

Dumbfounded, I stammered in prayer, *I'm doing the responsible things. I'm taking my medicine and getting help. In a few months, I should be better.* In the back of my mind, though, I deliberated, *What in the world? Is God asking me to ask Him to heal me? Isn't that backwards?*

Obviously, God heard both conversations.

In the awkward silence of my mind, I seemed to hear God's impatient fingers strumming the table in front of Him, waiting for my answer.

OK, will You heal me? The tone of voice in my head sounded rather perplexed.

The emphatic answer allowed no room for questions. "Yes," He said.

What just happened, and why?

Later in the evening, during my bedtime routine, I reached for my antidepressant medication. I jumped when God's stern voice startled me. "You did not believe me," he said.

Again, I found myself stammering to God. *Don't you know I can't do that? I can't just stop taking this medicine!* Realizing the futility of arguing with God, I saw the choice in front of me. If I believed He healed me, I no longer required the medication.

Trembling, I returned it to the shelf without a word. I made the choice, but my mind began a tirade of questions.

Have I lost my mind? No, I know that was God's voice. Why would He do this? J. won't believe me. I will scare him to death if I tell him.

He knows I need the meds. But wait, maybe I don't. Did God really just heal me?

Now, dear reader, let me stop here and be clear: Don't presume upon God, demand healing from Him, and stop taking your medicine. There's nothing sinful about being on antidepressants. With depression, your body lacks the chemicals necessary to think and feel clearly. It can be dangerous to abruptly stop taking them. It's perfectly okay to ask Him to heal you too, but don't try to force Him by discontinuing your medications. If He chooses to heal you, He will make it as clear to you as He did to me, in a way which makes sense to you.

God kept His promise. Throughout the next few weeks, my reasoning cleared, and my emotions stabilized. I began to see the damage caused in my marriage as a result of the depression, and I worked to make changes. Eventually, I told J. about my experience with God. It baffled him too, but he welcomed the difference it made in our home.

What an amazing blessing God gave me through His healing power. He restored my body, tended the wounds in our marriage, and brought happiness again to our home—just in time. We enjoyed those last few years immensely, and I am forever grateful for his unmerited gift to me.

In January 2005, merely two months after the accident, I scheduled an appointment with my gynecologist. My physical conditions demanded a hysterectomy, but my doctor worried about my emotional state. I assured him J. and I had made the decision together, beforehand. When he asked about remarriage, I told him I didn't intend to marry again quickly. If and when I did, I expected to be too old to consider giving birth to another child. The unfair timing of the surgery didn't change the reality of the situation.

. . . the doctor said I showed some "sophisticated defense mechanisms allowing me to absorb the pain at a measured rate."

The people handling my insurance for the accident required psychological testing before the surgery. They expected these tests to show symptoms of depression, requiring psychiatric care. However, the opposite proved true. Instead, the doctor said I showed some "sophisticated defense mechanisms allowing me to absorb the pain at a measured rate."

It amazed me as much as it amazed the doctors. I found myself telling the story to them. Maybe God healed me for a second reason: to tell of His goodness.

Am I willing?

Journal Entry: February 21, 2005

Can I be myself, hurts and all, with others?[62]

> *"Tyson and I were talking about sharing the pain and feelings publicly. He said for God to use what happened, I am going to have to be willing to share it all—even the darkest times, so that God can use it to help others. I said I was scared to do that. Then, he said 'You're going to have to get over that.' How frightening. How vulnerable. How selfless. God help me."*

Soon, I began to tell small pieces of my story. When people asked questions, I tried to answer honestly, without hiding my own wrestling. The more I shared, the more people desired to hear.

I decided if someone had the courage to ask, I would have the courage to answer.

It wasn't easy to talk about the night of the accident, but I *could* talk about the song God sang to me that night. One by one, I shared the story over and over. I sensed the miraculous story of hope in the middle of *my* disaster encouraged other people too. It comforted me.

Finally, one Sunday, I got brave enough to share the story with a larger group of people at my own church.

Journal Entry: February 27, 2005

The dark shadows of sorrow are dispelled by the light of hope.[63]

> *"Today, I sang for church, "Voice of Truth"[64] and shared how God sang it to me during the long hours the night of the accident. I was amazed. I felt God's presence so completely. I could hear my own voice, strong and gentle, like it was coming from someone else. Becky said she could hear both of my kid's voices in mine. What a sweet thing to say. I was able to share the story without crying. I even looked at the audience. I found myself smiling as I sang—do not be afraid! Truly God had taken away the fear! He replaced it with Hope. That's what it felt like. Hope."*

My wounded heart started to sing.

My wounded heart started to sing.

THE CURTAIN

I yearned to be able to view a memory movie of a day in our life—*any* day. I yearned to remember every exact word spoken. That, of course, was impossible, but it frustrated me to only remember bits and pieces.

So I begged God to help me remember more. His gentle response made me ache with sorrow. I couldn't emotionally handle the memories, but He promised they would come later. Reality soaked in. My heart lay shattered in a million pieces, but God protected the fragile fragments in the palm of His hand. Without His ability to mend them, my emotions were beyond repair.

One of our pastor friends told me, "There is a heavy curtain that has been drawn over your life right now, and all seems so dark, but, in His time, God's hand will begin to lift the curtain, and allow the light of His mercy and grace to flood your life with healing."

In time, his words proved true. The curtain raised inch by inch.

Several years later, I found myself speaking to a crowd of people in a Kansas church. I recognized several of the people sitting in the pews, including that pastor. I felt small in front of him. His influence in my life spanned many years and involved numerous roles—our pastor in college; our mentor during J.'s calling to ministry; our colleague while we served in Kansas and Nebraska; and one of the pastors who led my family's funeral. Now, *I* spoke in *his* church. When I finished sharing, I quickly took my seat while their pastor concluded the service.

Suddenly, my pastor friend slipped into the pew beside me. He leaned down and said, "The curtain has lifted. I can see God's light in you."

I wept.

At times during those long, hard years it didn't seem possible, but little by little the Light of Hope dawned in my life.

God never dropped a single piece of my heart, and He won't drop yours either. Lay the shattered remains of your heart in His capable, loving hands and give Him time to work.

Chapter 11

A WARMTH IN SOLITUDE

"Have I not commanded you? Be strong and courageous. Do not be terrified; do not be discouraged, for the Lord your God will be with you wherever you go."

JOSHUA 1:9

I sorted, packed, and labeled for six months. With the process complete, the next step became clear. Though I felt loved and protected in the parsonage, the church needed to begin seeking another pastor. So I chose a home and began the process of buying it. It boggled my mind to make the decisions alone, without my J.

TIME TO GO

My detailed preparations made moving day organizationally simple. I labeled each box with the location to put it. One wall of each room displayed a sketch of the furniture placement. I probably overcompensated with the physical process since nothing could prepare me for the emotional ache of leaving my home.

The love of my church family buoyed my courage to face the day. Their pickups lined the street. Each one waited to carry its precious cargo to the other place. Everyone scurried to work. In a few minutes, the rooms began to empty. Unable to watch, I drove to the new house and waited for the trucks to arrive.

By early afternoon, we completed the move—my clothes hung in the closet, every bed set up, and each dish in the cabinet. In the backyard, a well-built shed with a wooden floor held sacred treasures: my husband and children's personal belongings.

Each box carefully stacked. Labeled. Safe. Within reach. And still mine.

Five years passed before I gained the courage and emotional energy to open them again and make further decisions. In the meantime, it gave me comfort simply to call the memoirs mine.

FIRESIDE COMFORT

Now what?

Packing and sorting busied me for months. Now, with the move completed, what should I do with my days? Stare at the walls? No thank you. A job didn't seem plausible either. My mind continued to lack the capacity to concentrate.

Most of our married life, I worked solely at home or for our church. During our time in Miami, however, I worked for a local CPA firm as an accountant for about a year. The extra money enabled us to replace our old, hail-dented brown pickup truck with a newer, nicer model. Janessa, Jayden, and I breathed a collective sigh of relief. No more backfiring in front of the school.

I received an unexpected call from the same accounting firm, asking me to work a couple of weeks while someone took a vacation. Skeptical, but willing to try, I agreed.

Maybe I can do it.

The tasks ought to have been familiar, but I couldn't remember the steps. When I tried to concentrate, my mind refused. Simple responsibilities overwhelmed and confused me. I completed the two weeks but realized I shouldn't return to the workforce yet. Frustrated, I wondered when—or if—my muddled mind would clear again.

God provided through his people during this time, in myriads of ways. Someone in Miami opened an account for me at a bank.

Churches and individuals dropped money into the account. An anonymous person bought me a vehicle to drive.

It's incredible how faithful God is. I don't think we ought to be surprised by it, but I believe God loves it when we admire His work with astonishment. Overwhelming gratitude filled my soul for my God who made a way for me until I could return to the work force.

But the question remained: *Now what?*

While I pondered the query, I decided to build a fire in my fireplace. I loved to challenge myself to start it with only one match. So I crumpled some paper and placed a little kindling across the top. Lighting the match, I touched it to the folds until the tiny pieces ignited. Slowly, I added small pieces of wood until the flame caught them on fire. Within a few minutes, I placed larger pieces on top, blowing gently until the flames engulfed them. The crackling sounds relaxed my mind. I snuggled close to the fire and delighted in its comforting warmth.

God's love warmed me like the fire. It soothed my wounded soul. I sensed His presence there with me in ways I've never felt it—before or since. Each morning, I awoke and asked, "What are we doing today, God?" He told me each step and reminded me of anything I forgot.

One morning He even told me, "Take a shower." So I took a deep breath, climbed out of bed, showered, and dressed. Day by day He led me forward. When my keep-going-energy level plummeted, and I fell into despair, He brought someone to my door.

Time and again, God brought me people when I needed them. Sometimes they came for a few days, sometimes they just dropped by for a visit, and sometimes they took me to lunch. Nearly every day someone ate at least one meal with me. I'm forever grateful to the people who listened to the Lord's nudging. God knew what I required better than I did. He used others as His hands and feet to bring me comfort—right to my front door.

DISTRACTIONS FOR LONLINESS

Most of us avoid pain, and I'm no exception. If I can distract myself from loneliness and pain, I will. So I did. I spent time with people and filled my days with simple interaction which didn't require much of me. The local college became my hangout where I helped the Baptist Collegiate Ministry leaders develop relationships with the students. I chatted with friends over a meal, attended concerts, plays, football and softball games, along with every event at the church. It filled my time, and I attempted to let it fill my heart.

Journal Entry: April 29, 2005

"At the revival this week, the music leader said he believed God wanted him to tell me that the best years of my life are yet to come. My eyes filled with tears and my emotions were filled with a wide range of thought. I want the years ahead to be good, maybe even great. But how can the best years be without my children? How can that be? And how can I face life that will never be that good again? That is filled with always looking backward? Never as happy as I was? I cannot make either choice."

Alone, the sorrow settled around me and threatened to drown me. So I didn't spend much time by myself. In fact, when I became aware of a young lady who lacked a place to live, I invited her to live with me.

To others, I appeared to be doing very well, but from my perspective, my inability to be alone proved my weakness. An introvert by nature, I refueled by time alone. In the past, I always looked forward to the few hours I carved out for myself. It boosted my energy when I finished a quiet project on my own.

My favorite time, however, came *with* my family. Because we ministered to people through relationships, interactions with others filled our schedules. So we treasured the evenings when we watched a movie, played games, or even took a drive to look for our dream house by the lake.

Now, being alone sucked life out of me instead of breathing life into me. I still desired some quiet time to reflect—but not alone. My personality rules were changing—I no longer recognized myself.

HONESTY AND FORGIVENESS

When I left home as a young adult, college gave me the opportunity to change things about myself. I hoped to be adventurous, meet new people, and "find myself."

Then, overnight at 40 years old, I lost my identity. Like a teenager again, I struggled to understand life.

Who am I? How can I figure it out?

I quickly learned people relaxed around me when I smiled, but I didn't always want to smile. Sometimes I honestly portrayed my grief, even if it made those around me uncomfortable, but occasionally I put on a mask to make it easier for them. When I did, God urged me to be more transparent.

Journal Entry: June 12, 2005

Grief is a roller coaster of emotions. Highs and lows, lows and highs.[65]

> *"Sometimes I think I can fly. I feel God's presence surround me and I can smile up to Him and feel Him smiling back, or telling me a joke (like on the plane when I couldn't sleep and He said to get out my Bible and read, that always puts me to sleep! Very funny God!)*
>
> *But sometimes the depths of my sorrow are more than can be explained. My chest hurts and I can't feel God or hear Him. All I can do is sit and stare.*
>
> *Sometimes I want people, and sometimes I don't. Sometimes I don't, and yet I cry out to not be alone. How confusing!*
>
> *Hold on to me, God. Don't let go."*

Frustration grew inside of me. When I expressed it to God one night, my anger flashed hot toward Him. I expected Him to be upset with me, but instead, I literally felt His hand ruffle the hair on the top of my head. When I was a child, my brother touched my head to say he loved me. Perplexed, I talked with a friend about my experience. I told him God seemed to almost be pleased with me expressing anger to Him. My friend said, "Maybe that's because you were finally honest with Him."

Ouch.

The same problem had caused great difficulty in my marriage. When I got annoyed or disgusted about something, I usually tried to cover my feelings, especially when I *shouldn't* feel the way I *did* feel. From J.'s point of view, I simply lied to him. He knew me well, and saw my true emotions, regardless of what I said. Thus, he concluded I didn't trust him with the truth. In "protecting" our relationship from negative feelings, I actually caused them.

Honesty. What a simple word. What a difficult concept.

I pondered my past mistakes and wished for the chance to go back and do a few things again. Instead of remembering good memories, I sunk into reliving my past failures. But God didn't leave me drowning. He rescued me from the guilt through a unique experience.

All my life, strange dreams left me wondering, "Where in the world did *that* come from?" Usually silly, but occasionally frightening, familiar people and places mixed together with fictional characters and events. In my favorite repetitive childhood dream, Gilligan lived at my house and cleaned his clothes by getting into the washing machine himself. I never considered my crazy dreams to be meaningful, so it took me completely by surprise when God intervened in my life through a dream.

Although some of you may disagree with me, I think most dreams simply help our minds unwind at night. They aren't meant to make sense. At the same time, I believe God *can* use dreams to communicate with us. He certainly did in the Bible. Besides, when I'm asleep, I'm finally quiet enough to get the point! God doesn't play games with us, however, trying to make us guess if the dream came from Him or not. If He sent the message, He will make it clear.

He did.

The next morning, I remembered every detail of the dream: I sat in my truck at the parsonage, watching Jayden come down the street from school. In his arms, he held three of my collector plates from Bradford Exchange.

Why would a boy take fancy plates to school for show and tell?

When he got closer, the question didn't matter. I saw the tears streaming down his face. Immediately I guessed what happened. The plates came in sets of four, not three.

He ran to me, climbed onto my lap, and began to sob. I held him close until he quieted down. Then I whispered, "Jayden, don't you know that no old plate is ever going to change my love for you?"

I woke up.

Sorrow overwhelmed me. Longing to hold him, I sobbed for my son. The more I cried, the more real-life stories came to my mind of the times I did NOT act with compassion and tenderness toward my children. My mind swamped with situations I wished I had done differently—times I wish I would have said, "I'm sorry," rather than defending myself.

. . . I heard God's gentle voice say, "Lora, don't you know that no old sin is ever going to change my love for you?"

It's too late now.

Regrets filled my soul.

The sobs simply consumed me. I moved from room to room in tormented grief. Finally, laying on the couch, my weeping faded out of sheer exhaustion. Still whimpering and shaking, but quiet, I heard God's gentle voice say, "Lora, don't you know that no old sin is ever going to change my love for you?"

Sweet forgiveness washed over me and wrapped itself around the pain of my heart. Peace flooded my soul. Nothing restores life like the forgiveness of our Lord. By grace, I now freely walked without the shackles of sin around my ankles.

A DATE WITH GOD

Days turned into weeks. Time walked through my life. A different normal formed.

I spent a lot of time talking with God and reading the Bible. Joshua 1:9 says, "Have I not commanded you? Be strong and courageous. Do not be terrified; do not be discouraged, for the LORD your God will be with you wherever you go." I took the verse literally and talked aloud to God, as if He stood beside me.

One day I planned to go on a shopping trip to Joplin, Missouri. I didn't want to go alone, but no one accepted the invitation to join me. Finally, within my spirit, God's quiet voice said, "I'll go with you."

So I took a deep breath and said, "Okay, let's do this."

I climbed into the driver's seat and chatted aloud to my passenger, recounting memories of former trips with my family. When we finished the errands, He said, "Want to go to Shake's?" I burst out laughing. One of my children's favorite places to go in Joplin was Shake's Frozen Custard. We loved their Chocolate Chip Cookie Dough Concrete, full of cookie dough so thick you can turn it upside down.

"Yum! Yes, let's go!"

So off we drove to Shake's. I didn't buy God His own custard. He enjoyed mine with me. Suddenly, I realized God and I were on a date.

We both loved it.

I don't know why God chooses to interact with us. I only know He does. His act of kindness and love sang to my wounded soul.

The radio played "Who Am I?"[66] by Casting Crowns. It expressed my awe and gratitude for my God, who loved me enough to take me on an ice cream date.

Who am I, that the Lord of all the earth
Would care to know my name, would care to feel my hurt?
Who am I, that the Bright and Morning Star
Would choose to light the way for my ever-wandering heart?

Who am I, that the eyes that see my sin
Would look on me with love and watch me rise again?
Who am I, that the voice that calmed the sea
Would call out through the rain and calm the storm in me?

Not because of who I am
But because of what You've done

Not because of what I've done
But because of who You are

I am a flower quickly fading, here today and gone tomorrow.
A wave tossed in the ocean. A vapor in the wind.
Still You hear me when I'm calling.
Lord, You catch me when I'm falling.
And You've told me who I am.

I am yours.[67]

Sometimes I actually miss those first months after the accident. It probably sounds crazy, but the intensity of my interaction with God during that time solidified my faith. Certainly, many days I wandered lost and confused, but other times His crystal-clear voice shattered my doubts. Today I rely upon those words for my life's foundation.

I *know* God is real. I am His and He is mine.

Will you trust Him too?

Chapter 12

A SOURCE OF STRENGTH

". . . we have this treasure in jars of clay to show that this all-surpassing power is from God and not from us."

II CORINTHIANS 4:7

When I was very young, my mom gave me a children's pop-up book of the Biblical story of Esther. When I opened it, a palace lifted off the page, and little paper dolls became the king and the queens, the hero and the villain. As I turned those pages, I imagined her life. I loved to read the story and act it out with the dolls, imagining the world of a princess. As a child, I skipped right over the tragedies of her story in the security of my world, but they spoke to me anew as a grieving adult.

RESISTING BITTERNESS

War consumed Esther's family history. Babylon conquered her native country of Israel and deported her great-grandparents to another land. The battles continued among nations until the Persians defeated the Babylonians almost fifty years later. Although the new regime allowed some of the Jews to return home, Esther's family remained in Susa. By the time Esther entered the world, Persia controlled 127 provinces.

Although the Bible doesn't indicate the specifics, tragedy entered Esther's young life claiming the lives of both her mother and father. During the cruel turn of events, however, God intervened and provided a man of faith to care for the little girl. Her cousin Mordecai took her in to be his own daughter.

Just when she found a new normal, life changed again with some unforeseen events.

Xerxes, the Persian King, became displeased with his wife and tossed her out of the palace. When he grew lonely, his attendants advised him to "gather" the beautiful young women from across the kingdom and choose a new queen. Esther was one of those beauties.

At the whim of a king, Esther lost her freedom.

In the moments before they took her to be prepared to meet the king, Mordecai forbid her to tell anyone of her Jewish heritage. He feared for her. Esther kept the promise, but in doing so, she lost her heritage and her family connection to Mordecai.

She lost her family—again.

Esther entered a world unlike her own. In my childhood naive mind, it looked like she'd entered a fairy-tale world, but for Esther, it was a world where innocence had vanished. Throughout the next year, each girl received luxurious beauty treatments—followed by one night with the king. Afterward, they became a permanent part of the king's harem. The process continued until someone won his affections and thus became queen.

Unable to control her own life's circumstances, she chose between becoming bitter or becoming beautiful, quite literally.

The situation gave cause for vicious anger, but she didn't let the anger turn to bitterness within her soul. Instead, she chose to grow in beauty. She learned about cosmetics and oils, followed the advice of the man in charge of the harem, and prepared to win the attention of the king. Her internal choice showed on her face. The scripture says, "Esther won the favor of everyone who saw her" (Esther 2:15b). Her inner beauty added to her outer beauty, and sure enough, the king chose her to be the next queen.

If Esther had chosen bitterness, she probably would have spent the rest of her life in the secondary palace, simply one of the harem. Then she wouldn't have been where God needed her to be, later in the story.[68]

Esther's story radically differs from mine, but I identify with suddenly being left without a family. When I read her story again, following the accident, I pondered her choice of beauty instead of bitterness.

Can I make the same choice? I sense the sharp edge of bitterness creeping into my heart.

One day I went to a family reunion with several of my family members. When we left the reunion, we each headed in our own directions in our separate vehicles. I prayed aloud in my truck, "Protect us, Lord, while we travel home." Instantly, deep within me rose the angry questions.

As the hot tears dripped down my cheeks, I recognized the choice in front of me: bitterness or beauty.

What difference does it make to pray? We prayed as we left Miami to go home, and what good did it do us? God will do whatever He wants to anyway!

As the hot tears dripped down my cheeks, I recognized the choice in front of me: bitterness or beauty.

The debate continued within me: Satan's loud, ugly accusations of the uselessness of faith, and God's soft voice reassuring me of His love.

If I let my anger turn to bitterness and destroy my faith, where does the path ahead lead? God has been the source of my peace and comfort. I don't want to leave Him. If I keep honestly praying and trying to live in this land without my family, like Esther did, where does that path lead? Maybe, just maybe, I'll be where God wants me to be, later in my *story.*

CRUX TIME

Sometime following Esther's coronation, a villain slithered into the palace by way of a promotion to the highest office in the king's court. His name was Haman and he flaunted his newfound power. When the king required the other officials to bow in Haman's presence, his ego grew exponentially.

One member of the council refused to bow down to Haman when he walked by. A Jew bowed solely to God, not to man.

That Jewish man was Mordecai.

Haman grew so angry he almost lost his mind in fury. His bitterness boiled until it became something entirely out of control. It bubbled inside him until the whole thing erupted into a plan to destroy Mordecai—and his entire race.

Angry, bitter people do irrational things.

A throw of the dice determined the day for every Jewish person to die. Haman made the death date into an edict, and posted it everywhere, in every language of the kingdom. I can only imagine the shock and agony which gripped the Jewish people.

Insulated behind the palace walls, Esther knew nothing of Haman's plan. Mordecai sent a message to her to warn her, and to plea for her help. He asked her to go to the king, tell him of her heritage, and plead for their lives.

Fear of failure can be paralyzing.

Mordecai's words stunned Esther. Her mind reeled with panic. What should she do? No one, not even his wife, entered the king's court without invitation. Nor did they try. The results of going to the king without being summoned came swift and deadly: the guard at the door simply cut off your head, no questions asked. No one but the king could intervene—that is IF he noticed in time and lifted his scepter before the guard lifted his sword.

She had not been summoned for thirty days.

Mordecai's second message to the queen said. "Do not think that because you are in the king's house you alone of all the Jews will escape. For if you remain silent at this time, relief and deliverance for the Jews will arise from another place, but you and your father's family will perish. And who knows but that you have come to royal position for such a time as this?" (Esther 4:13-14).

The words of the note from her beloved cousin Mordecai caused a gigantic lump to form in her throat. Her love for him and her family dropped her to her knees. With her parents already dead, the anticipated destruction of her entire people group surely drove her to despair. I wonder which frightened her more: dying, or failing to rescue her people?

Fear of failure can be paralyzing.

The enemy sought to destroy the Jews, but God planned for their rescue ahead of time. A young orphan girl, stolen from her second home with her cousin, found herself in the position to make a difference. What would she do?

She prayed—and asked others to pray with her. For three days, the queen and her maidens abstained from eating and drinking with the purpose of undistracted prayer. Esther asked Mordecai and the Jews to do the same. She determined to hear from God—but not alone.[69]

PRAYERS OF OTHERS

The prayers of others sustained me after the accident. Sometimes I clearly heard from God, and I clung to those words. Often, God used the language of music to penetrate the pain of my heart. But my weak, wounded, traumatized mind only processed simple thoughts. Without question, the prayers of God's faithful people kept me from sinking into an abyss of pain from which I might not return.

Journal Entry: July 10, 2005

In this season of sorrow we may turn from God, but He does not turn from us.[70]

> *"I am so grateful that God didn't give up on me. I had this picture in my mind of how close I would be to God by now, talking to Him almost all the time. After all, He was supposed to become my husband. The truth has instead been lack of prayer, short attention span and distraction. I've had to rely on other's prayers for me because I can't pray. (It really makes me realize how vital intercessory prayer is) . . ."*

I admire Esther. She didn't rely on her own faith alone. Instead, she leaned into the faith of others, asking them to pray for and with her. She told them exactly what she lacked. It's always been difficult for me to ask for help. Instead, I encouraged others to rely on me. To my shame, I even took pride in my faith, seldom admitting my need for help.

. . . I even took pride in my faith, seldom admitting my need for help.

When I lost my family, I saw the truth: my faith was weak. It's easy to believe in God when life gives me blessings and God's assignments are simple. But when the enemy threatens to destroy me, and the assignment appears impossible, and I am not sure my own faith will hold, I need people with faith surrounding me, praying for me and with me. Perhaps I always did, even if I didn't admit it.

Today, I continue to lean on others to help me pray. A treasured group of prayer warriors hear from me regularly. I share my concerns, frustrations, and victories with them. When I face a big decision in my life, I do not do it alone. I ask others to pray and listen with me, like Esther did.

OBEDIENT COURAGE

When Esther heard God's answers, she followed his simple instructions to the letter, even though the risk frightened her. Her faith gave her the courage to act, even in her fear. With a deep breath, she headed to the palace throne room door.

The moment he saw her, he raised his scepter.

Inwardly relieved, she approached the king with dignity. When he asked what she requested, she simply invited him to a banquet she made ready and asked him to bring his top court official. The king agreed and called for Haman.[71]

I admire Esther's courage. She probably didn't *feel* brave or strong, even if she looked the part.

From the beginning, people continually told me, "You are a strong woman." The statement amazed me. I didn't think clearly enough to hold a job. Decisions about the future eluded me. Tomorrow seemed long term. I relied on others to lead me through the financial and legal decisions step-by-step. People took care of me, quite literally in every area of my life. Yet they described me as strong. I simply didn't understand it—I had never felt so weak in my life.

One day I responded to someone. "All I'm doing is getting up and getting dressed."

They said, "That's amazing. I think I would just stay in bed."

I sighed. It seemed impossible to convince anyone of my weakness.

My mom helped me understand from the other's perspective. She said, "They see God's strength in you."

An image formed in my mind. If I stored diamonds in a glass jar, no one would look at the jar and exclaim, "What a pretty jar!" No, they would observe the sparkle, reflecting in the glass and gasp at the beauty of the diamonds. Isn't it funny we attribute God's character to the person reflecting it?

I reminisced about our younger days. My husband and I thought if God gave us the chance, we could do anything for Him. We felt invincible and strong of spirit. Interestingly, I don't remember anyone ever complimenting us on our strength. Idealistic might describe us better.

Now, I *know* I'm helpless without Him. With my pride out of the way, God's strength can be clearly seen in my weakness. The Bible says in II Corinthians 4:7, "But we have this treasure in jars of clay [our earthly body] to show that this all-surpassing power is from God, and not from us."

The next time someone commented on my strength, I finally knew what to say. "No, but I have a strong God."

Courage isn't bravery or strength. It's the choice to act even when I am afraid since I trust Someone who has no need to be afraid. It's trusting *His* strength and power will hold me up when there's nothing left of mine. It's getting out of bed in the morning when there's nothing to motivate me because I believe God still lives and loves me enough to intervene on my behalf. That's what Esther did. She walked forward with faith-filled courage into the banquet.

In the dining room, the story takes a significant twist. When the king asked what Esther requested from them, she merely invited them to another banquet the next day and promised to answer the question there. Now at first glance, the story reader might reason Esther simply chickened out and bought herself some more time, but I don't think so. God's amazing plan unfolded when she followed the specific, unusual instructions God gave her while she prayed.

Haman left the banquet filled with cocky pride. I picture him strutting down the road, full of himself, over-impressed with his good fortune. The king and queen invited *him* to a private banquet. His ego inflated his hat size another notch.

Full of himself, he passed through the king's gate where the other officials sat. Mordecai did not rise to show respect, nor bow in his presence. In fact, he didn't even appear to fear Haman. How? Why? Haman concocted his plan not only to kill Mordecai and his people in the future, but to make him agonize in the present. Why did the scheme not work? Rage filled him. He wanted Mordecai to grovel at his feet.

Haman's wife and pals listened as he spewed out the story. They consoled him and helped him add to his evil plan. Haman ordered gallows built and purposed to ask the king for permission to hang Mordecai tomorrow. Why wait until the day the law designated? Hang the enemy, then go enjoy the banquet with the king and queen!

That night, the king couldn't sleep. He called in a servant to read the royal diaries to him. (Interesting sleep aid.) In a twist designed by God, the servant read a story about a man who uncovered a plot to kill the king. The king pondered the story and inquired if the man received any honor for his service. His assistant researched the answer. No. None.

The man's name? Mordecai.

Early the next morning, the king considered how to *honor* Mordecai at the same time Haman arrived in the inner court to ask to *hang* Mordecai. Upon seeing Haman in the entryway, the king invited him in and asked this question, "What should be done for the man the king delights to honor?" (Esther 6:6).

It makes me laugh, absolutely every time I read this. Haman's unbelievable conceit makes him say to himself, "Who is there that the king would rather honor than me?" (Esther 6:6). With pleasure, he gave the king his best, most extravagant idea.

". . . have them bring a royal robe the king has worn and a horse the king has ridden, one with a royal crest placed on its head. Then let the robe and horse be entrusted to one of the king's most noble princes. Let them robe the man the king delights to honor, and lead him on the horse through the city streets, proclaiming before him, 'This is what is done for the man the king delights to honor!'" (Esther 6:8-9).

The king loved the idea—and sent Haman to do this for Mordecai.

Wow.

Imagine the ironic humiliation Haman endured. He walked through the streets, glorifying Mordecai in front of the same friends who helped him build gallows for him the prior night. Then, as soon as he arrived back to the palace, before he could realign his facade, the dinner bell rang for the second banquet with the king and queen.

This time, the queen told the king about how her people were singled out to be killed—by Haman.

The king hung Haman on the same gallows he had built for Mordecai, and the Jewish people celebrated their salvation. God intervened on behalf of his people.[72]

If Esther ever questioned why God allowed these awful things to happen to her, she now knew her answer. God chose her for an important job, and she courageously chose to trust the plan.

I suppose everyone seeks to find a significant reason for the events which happen in their lives. Esther's life fulfilled a vital role in the life of an entire country. Even though it took a long time, she eventually recognized that her loss put her in the right place at the right time for God's purpose.

What about me?

People often told me, "God has a big purpose for you. There must be some significant reason He left you on this earth." The story of Esther gave significant credibility to the idea. At first, I became angry. Nothing could be a big enough reason to warrant taking my entire family away from me. But slowly, over time, the anger gave way to a twisted resolve.

If I can figure out my assignment, and get it done, maybe God will let me die too.

In the following months, however, God chipped away at my plan through Esther's story. An unusual thought unsettled me. Even after she saved the nation, nothing significantly changed in her situation. She was still queen to a Persian king instead of being free to choose her own prince. Her parents still wouldn't be there to hold her babies. Nothing about her life resembled the simplicity she once experienced. She needed to find meaningful life in her present circumstances.

With a deep sigh I whispered, "So do I."

Step-by-step, I began to understand what God truly desires from me: a *daily* relationship with Him. The enjoyment of His presence sustains me, though I cannot physically see Him yet. One day I will walk to the throne room door and be welcomed into the presence of the King. What a glorious day! My present encouragement comes in knowing He's mine. When I lose sight of Him and seek something more, I lose the very essence of joy. His daily presence brings the meaningful life I desire.

The more I learn about God's character, the more I can share with others. God gave me opportunities to talk about my faith almost immediately. With the help of my prayer warriors, I found courage to speak. One by one, I answered people's questions, and encouraged them to believe God truly exists.

Esther could have moped around for the rest of her life completely separated from her family and her God. Instead, she chose to resist bitterness, lean into the faith of others, and courageously obey the plan of her God. As a result, a plot to eradicate an entire nation failed, her cousin became the highest official in the king's court[73], and she found the joy of living.

I want to be like Esther.

Chapter 13

A CHALLENGE TO SHARE

"For everything that was written in the past was written to teach us, so that through endurance and the encouragement of the Scriptures we might have hope."

ROMANS 15:4

Over the years, J. went to Brazil several times on mission trips with a group called Pioneer Missions. They helped to build church buildings for groups of believers without one. Brazil easily became J.'s passion. He enjoyed traveling in the beautiful country and fell in love with the Brazilian people. My husband planned to join the team every year for the rest of his life.

I guess he did.

SHARING PAIN

It took me a couple of years to gather the courage to go with him. Once I did, I saw what captivated him. Even though we didn't speak their language, we chatted through interpreters, and I enjoyed learning a little Portuguese. Our mutual love for the Lord made it easy to become friends. J. made the yearly trip once on his own, then we went twice together. Each time we built a church building in a different city, but the Pioneer Mission team often included the same people, both from the United States and from Brazil. We anticipated seeing our friends each year on the trip.

On my third year, I felt clear conviction to stay home. Without understanding why, I let J. go on to Brazil without me. Instead, I traveled with our kids in the states while their Daddy worked in another country. We drove to Liberal to see grandparents, and we visited friends in our former communities: Clay Center, Kansas, and Grand Island, Nebraska.

Laughter filled our van as we roamed from place to place.

A few months later I understood why God encouraged me to stay home from Brazil. It was my last summer with my kids. I'm grateful for the precious memories of those two weeks of adventure together.

The next summer, the first after the accident, I felt the need to return to Brazil one more time. This time to honor J.'s life among the Brazilian people and the Pioneer Missions team. It humbled me to represent J. on the trip. I loved hearing memories of J. from the team. We laughed and cried together while I shared family pictures and videos. It made me glad to hear they remembered J., and treasured him too.

This particular mission trip allowed me the opportunity to extend my visit by arriving before the rest of the building team. Those who came early volunteered at an orphanage. The kids were precious, but I struggled to walk among them without tears.

Journal Entry: July 30, 2005

> *"Last night we arrived at the orphanage. I felt so out of place. I don't know where I fit in. We toured the area on foot, heard the dreams for the orphanage, and played with the boys. When one of them attacked me and another boy with a water gun, the one on my lap buried his face in my shoulder. My heart absolutely broke. I carried him a long time until my heart could no longer handle it. I put him down and left. I went back to my room and wept long and hard.*

When I finally came out, the pastor met me with a little boy in tow. He had him apologize for squirting me with the water gun. I felt horrible. They had misunderstood my tears. I hadn't realized they could see my pain before I left them. I guess I'm not such a good coverup."

The child didn't deserve the blame for my tears. I hurried to find a translator and for the first time at the orphanage, I began to explain what happened to my family.

By suppertime, the news spread throughout the orphanage. Child after child hugged me. One of the boys told me, "We be your family." These children understood the depth of my pain from experience.

Truly, suffering understands suffering. I wondered why I struggled to share my pain with the children who so easily understood. I think my pain contained a degree of selfishness. To share it with another person who also hurts acknowledged they hurt as badly as I did. Part of me refused to admit that truth yet.

. . . my pain contained a degree of selfishness. To share it with another person who also hurts acknowledged they hurt as badly as I did. Part of me refused to admit that truth yet.

The boys ran and played and laughed together. They created a family together, despite their pain. They were finding a new life. Like Esther's story, the orphans challenged me to do the same. Again, I struggled with the willingness to try.

I watched some of our team members fall in love with the boys, some even wishing to take one home with them to the States. My heart pushed back against the thought. I wondered why. Perhaps I simply placed boundaries up so I wouldn't love another child and risk being hurt again. Then one night, the lightbulb came on in my mind. There *was* a group of young people I loved deeply and desired to keep close to me.

My children's friends.

Journal Entry: August 20, 2005

"I've decided that one of the main blessings of this trip is that I want to go home. Homesickness . . . imagine that as a blessing! But it really is—because I desire to be there, to start walking toward life."

Once home, I hugged every teen I found, grateful to feel the love flow in me again. My emotions continued to bounce up and down, for the time being. Later, when I became willing to hear it, those who traveled before me through pain helped me walk toward hope.

SHARING JANESSA'S WORDS

Janessa's written words impacted many people in a variety of ways. When I found one of her Bible studies from her last year at camp, I let her youth pastor, Tyson, read it. She learned a great deal from his teaching and it showed in her writing. The words encouraged him, and he began to dream about the impact her words might have on her youth group.

When the time came for camp the following year, Tyson put feet to his dream. Each year, the campers competed in a T-shirt design contest using the camp theme. This year, however, he chose to use Janessa's words from last year's Bible study for the group's shirt. It didn't necessarily fit with the theme for the year, and probably wouldn't qualify for the contest, but the impact of her words on her friends interested him more than the possible award.

We found a local printer who lifted Janessa's handwriting off the page and printed it on the shirt. Her signature from another journal perfectly completed the quote.

On the front, the design simply said, "*Be Different.*"

On the back, Janessa's words read, *"Ya know, no matter where I go, or what I do, there's always going to be someone who hates me or thinks I'm just really weird. So why not take it and run w/ it. Since they already think I'm different, why not tell them about God. Maybe then they will be different w/ me."*

Falls Creek Conference Center registered about 6,500 campers the week our church attended. Our youth proudly wore their shirts and shared Janessa's story with anyone who stopped to notice. True to Tyson's expectations, her words impacted everyone who read them. Soon, the leaders of the camp asked about it, and to our surprise chose our shirt to be the overall winner of the contest. The youth group cheered when her shirt appeared on the screen during the evening service. My heart swelled with pride and gratitude.

When we returned home, the kids continued to wear their shirts. Soon, word spread, and people asked to buy one. We reprinted again and again. A local Christian bookstore even carried them for a time, along with a card pointing customers to a website with her story. I remained astounded.

The epitome of the experience came for me one day on the Northeastern Oklahoma A&M College campus in Miami. I volunteered to help on Welcome Day. One of the new students wore Janessa's shirt. Since we didn't know her, one of the ladies with me asked her if she knew the story of the girl on the shirt. She said she read about her at the bookstore. Then my friend introduced me as "Janessa's mom." No greater honor exists. With tears of pride and joy, I embraced the young woman wearing my daughter's words.

Janessa lived her faith "out loud," unashamed to talk about her God or her faith. In 2005, Casting Crowns released a song called "Lifesong."[74] It reminded me of Janessa and challenged me to make my life a song of praise to God, like she did.

Lord I give my life
A living sacrifice
To reach a world in need
To be your hands and feet
So may the words I say
And the things I do
Make my lifesong sing
Bring a smile to you[75]

As a child, Janessa's faith in the Word of God encouraged me to believe in the possibility of miraculous healing. Now, her words spurred me forward once again. This time, she urged me to "take it and run with it." When my faith grew stronger, I hoped to be God's hands and feet, bringing a message of hope to those who thought they could never believe again.

SHARING MY HOME

Tyson understood I needed encouragement to be involved in ministry. So, in the fall of 2005, he asked me to consider teaching a Bible study to the college students who attended our church. Since this included only three young adults, this seemed to be feasible for me. I agreed.

I still didn't grasp the magnitude of my story in our small town. When I arrived for the first Bible study expecting three kids, I found a room full of young people from the college who heard about my story and came to learn more about me and the God who kept me alive.

There began something big. Not in terms of numbers, but in terms of finding a piece of my heart again. Most of these young men and women did not know my family personally. They only knew me. Being with them gave me a small taste of what, for me, became a new identity. *I* did not know Lora without J., Janessa, and Jayden. They helped me find her.

Small town kids, who came to the "big city" of Miami to go to a two-year college, they hoped to find a place that reminded them of home. On a whim, I told them they could do their laundry at my house. Nothing opens the door to ministry like a free washer and dryer. They began to come. The shelf in my laundry room filled with various detergents, each with a name printed down the side. While their laundry washed, they worked on homework, played games with me, or simply chatted about everything from daily college life to deep faith questions.

These kids wanted interaction—God's healing gift to me.

One day, one of them said, "Hey, if we bring the food, can we cook dinner for you at your house while the laundry is washing?"

I stammered a shocked yes.

That began a traditional Monday night meal, often with as many as fifteen to twenty students there. We picked the theme together, and the kids brought ingredients to add to mine. Everyone worked together to make a meal. Some cooked, some grilled, some washed the dishes, some cleaned the gutters, and some emptied the old coals from the fireplace. When the meal concluded, we played together. The backyard became a great place to jump on the trampoline or climb trees. My kitchen table filled with kids playing cards or became the center of some great debate about current events. In the living room, kids relaxed on the floor, or worked on homework in front of the comforting fire. Music played from the sound system, but the television remained silent. These kids wanted interaction—God's healing gift to me.

My neighbors worried about me. They expressed concern the kids might take advantage of me. When I said they cook supper and clean out the gutters, they stared at me, speechless. I waited until they walked away to burst out laughing.

Laughter.

The faintly familiar sound surprised me.

Thanksgiving 2005, the students said, "Let's have a 'real' Thanksgiving meal together!" So we did—turkey, dressing, mashed potatoes and gravy—everything. We peeled an entire twenty-pound bag of potatoes into the garbage disposal.

My washer ran quietly in the background. Load after load of students' laundry being cleaned.

The meal tasted wonderful. We enjoyed every bite. Then, during a lull in conversation, someone noticed the sound of running water coming from the laundry room. Everyone ran to look. Water sprayed two-feet high behind the washer. Soon someone yelled from the bathroom. Water bubbled out of the bathtub drain. At the same time, water started spewing out of the sink in the kitchen. When we turned off the washer, the fountains stopped, but the drains didn't allow the water to escape. Dirty dishes and smelly water filled the sink. We wondered if potato peelings floated in the washer water.

I called my plumber friend. He couldn't come until the next morning. Meanwhile, we left the dishes and enjoyed the evening together.

It took three days to clean up the mess! I found an old "I Love Lucy" cartoon clipping with the washer spraying water out the top of it and used packing tape to put it on top of my washing machine. It's still there to this day. Every time one of my "kids" comes to visit, they laugh with me about it.

They still come to visit—over ten years later. We hold reunions in Oklahoma in the fall, meeting wherever we can find a place big enough for all the spouses and children who now come with them. Occasionally, a smaller group even makes the 400-mile journey to where I live now. Their presence continues to spread God's healing balm on my wounded soul.

SHARING FORGIVENESS

Several months following the accident, I traveled through Wichita on my way home from Liberal. When I pass Glenn Stark's buffalo sculptures on the hill East of Kingman, my mind always pauses to remember. In the valley below the buffaloes, our van came to rest after the collision. This time, I considered the man in the other vehicle on the night of the accident. The memory of his tears always stays on the edge of my mind. I wondered how he fared, both physically and emotionally. Someday, I hoped to meet him and tell him I am not angry with him.

. . . I felt the Holy Spirit nudge me and say, "Today."

While I pondered what he might be going through, I felt the Holy Spirit nudge me and say, "Today." My mind sputtered with the prospect of trying to find him. What should I say? When I realized my notebook with his contact information laid on the floorboard of my truck, I knew I heard God correctly.

Do it now.

When I reached Wichita, I pulled into a fast-food parking lot and opened my phone. Taking a deep breath, I dialed. A woman answered. The words stuck in my throat when I opened my mouth to speak. I took a jagged deep breath and said, "Hello . . . this is Lora Jones."

She took an audible deep breath too, and said, "Hello." I fumbled around a bit, but I asked if I might come and visit. She said she would talk to her husband and call me right back.

Trying to swallow my burger proved rather futile. Time stood still. When the phone rang, I jumped. With a sigh of relief, I heard her say it was okay to come. She gave me directions, and I headed toward their home.

I had no earthly idea what to say. I just wanted him to know I didn't hate him and I didn't want him to hate himself.

Parking across the street from the house, I took another shaky breath and got out of the truck. Without further thought, I walked toward his house. In front of me, stood a middle-aged, clean-shaven man. Relying on crutches to maneuver, he opened the screen door, leaned against it, and waited for me. I peered into his sad eyes. He looked straight into mine and opened both arms to me.

I fell into his arms and we wept together.

It will always amaze me he took the risk to hug me. He didn't wait to see why I came or hear what I planned to say. His embrace spoke without words, his deep sorrow for my broken heart. My presence whispered the words I hoped to say and opened the door for conversation.

We talked a long, long time that day, and many more times in the years to come. We became friends—friends who met by accident. Together, we walk toward hope.

Part 4

SHARE THE STORY

Chapter 14
SORROW AND JOY

"See, I am doing a new thing! Now it springs up; do you not perceive it?"

ISAIAH 43:19

At times when I've heard God, I've preferred to pretend I didn't.

The more I lived my grief "out loud," the more people asked me to share. At first, I spoke in very simple ways—a five-minute testimony during a worship service, or a solo for my own church. But within a year, people were asking me to speak in more formal ways.

SURRENDER

One of the first invitations came from my home church in Liberal. Their pastor repeatedly asked me to share my story when I felt ready. I easily put him off with "I'm not ready." Each time he called, God nudged me forward like a hesitant child in her first school program. He urged me to start sharing more publicly, but it overwhelmed me. I back-peddled against the idea. What could I say? Surely, I should wait until He answered more of my many questions!

In January 2006, fourteen months after the accident, my husband's grandmother passed away. I drove to her funeral. During the entire eight-hour drive, God urged me to say yes to First Baptist, and I argued the whole way.

The plan didn't make sense to me. I *loved* to lead Bible studies. It fits me to sit at a table and lead a group of people to consider the scripture. I asked people questions designed to help them in their daily life with Christ. When the group shared, they learned from each other. On the other hand, I *hated* standing alone in front of people. I don't think quickly on my feet and deciding what to say comes even slower than my thoughts. Frankly, I survived public speaking in college by the skin of my teeth, with great fear and trepidation!

Can't I just continue talking with people one-on-one at the café or go back to teaching Sunday School? Why do I need to stand in front of people and do all the talking?

The gravity of this decision weighed heavily in my gut. It loomed bigger than being willing to speak at my home church, which scared me enough, honestly. What if this assignment from God went beyond First Baptist? Deep within me, I sensed it would. God insisted. Relentlessly.

When I arrived at the small town in Kansas for the funeral, I had yet to reach any conclusions about sharing my story in a more public way. I walked into the sanctuary of the small church and tried to focus above the turmoil of my spirit. The pastor took his place on the stage and began to tell about our beautiful, kind Grandma Beulah. Then, he said something which made time stop for me. He said, "I've never used this Scripture for a funeral before, but I know God wanted me to use it today." The Scripture from Isaiah 43:19 read, "See, I am doing a new thing! Now it springs up; do you not perceive it?"

I looked to the heavens.

Seriously? You are going to preach to me during Grandma's funeral? This is supposed to be about Grandma! That's not fair!

I no longer listened to what the pastor said. God's voice spoke too loudly inside my head. "Don't you get it, Lora? I'm going to do something new through you!"

The service ended, and we headed to the graveside. Emotions overcame me, and I retreated to a vehicle by myself. Eventually I crawled into the back of the van to retrieve my calendar from my purse. I resigned myself to obey.

OKAY, OKAY, I'll go. When do I have to go?

As I pulled out the calendar, I saw my phone's light blinking. In a last-ditch effort to distract myself from God, I told Him, *Hold on a minute, I have a message on my phone.*

Boy, I am one stubborn woman!

It didn't distract God. He had one more thing to say.

I listened to the message. You aren't going to believe this anymore than I did. The message came from a lady in Pittsburg, Kansas. She said, "I understand you are a speaker. Would you be willing to share at our upcoming women's event?"

Dumbfounded, I stared at the phone. Speechless. In the quiet, God said, "This is going to be intense and short term."

Dropping my head, I whispered, "*Okay.*"

When I got home from the trip, a letter waited in my mailbox from a friend. J. and I attended seminary with him. In his letter, he said he planned (before the accident) to invite J. to come and preach a revival at his church. Now, he felt urged by God to invite me to come and speak at their women's retreat.

I stared at the letter shaking in my hands. It contained the third confirmation of God's call to speak. The sermon from the pastor at Grandma's funeral; a phone call from a woman I'd never met; and a letter from an old friend, each confirmed what I heard deep within me. None of them realized the power of their words.

God's serious. This is going to happen. What in the world am I going to say?

Yes.

TELL THE STORY

When I asked God what to share, He said, "Tell the story." The words of one of my favorite hymns came to me, reminding me of how much "I Love to Tell the Story."[76]

I love to tell the story Of unseen things above,
Of Jesus and his glory, Of Jesus and his love:

I love to tell the story Because I know 'tis true;
It satisfies my longings As nothing else can do.[77]

"Tell the story," God said. I knew how to tell stories. That made it seem much easier.

I loved to read stories to children and watch their reactions to the characters. My children listened to me read to them nearly every night their whole lives. J. used to tease me sometimes about the extensive process of getting them ready for bed. Together we read a book or two, then I tucked them in, often talking awhile with each one. I planned to follow the routine as long as they enjoyed it. Time flies by quickly, and before long, I knew they would be off on their own. I have many regrets about things I wish I did differently, but that is not one of them. The memory of stories at bedtime has a cherished place in my heart.

We read stories of adventure. We read biographies. We read fiction. We read the true stories of the Bible. The lessons of the Scriptures came alive in the characters. Even now, no matter how often I read the stories, I can always learn something fresh by reading them again.

I lacked wisdom, and the answers to life's questions, but I knew stories of God's presence in my life. Perhaps I could encourage someone else along the way to believe God has an active part in their life too.

So I started sharing in worship services, women's retreats, and events. I told of God's powerful presence the night of the accident, sang the songs He sang to me, and expressed the lessons I learned, as God revealed them. The story of the accident drained me, but retelling the stories of the presence of God kept me focused on Him. It gave me purpose. I love to tell the story of God.

God described it accurately—intense and short lived. I received forty invitations in the next fifteen months.

I love to tell the story; 'Tis pleasant to repeat
What seems, each time I tell it, More wonderfully sweet:
I love to tell the story, For some have never heard

The message of salvation From God's own holy Word.[78]

I prayed my story helped others understand His love for them, maybe for the first time. Even believers sometimes forget what they've seen Him do, so I hoped my story helped them remember their own journey with the Lord.

I love to tell the story; For those who know it best
Seem hungering and thirsting To hear it, like the rest:
And when, in scenes of glory, I sing the new, new song,
'Twill be the old, old story That I have loved so long.[79]

Our life stories connect us to each other. When I picture heaven, I imagine going from person to person listening to each life story. What joy it will be to hear their stories and to tell mine. From heaven's perspective, we will be able to see how our stories intertwined with each other, and what God did with our lives which we didn't understand when we were merely mortal.

HEALING THE HEART

The more often I spoke, the more my eyes opened to the pain of others. Some cried for me, but most shed tears from their own pain. Weary eyes reflected pain-filled souls. That year I met dozens, maybe hundreds, of men and women who had buried their children and grandchildren or lost their children in a multitude of other ways. Everyone told me the same thing: "The pain of losing a child will never go away."

I shared my story with them and told them of my confidence in God's existence and love. Never in my life had I been more certain of my faith. But I wanted to tell them how to make it through the pain, and I didn't know how.

The fact glared at me. Our pain doesn't end. I saw it in my Mom's eyes.

In 1994, my father died. I stayed with my mom for a while after everyone else went home. During the week, Mom talked about my brother Keith more than I had ever heard her talk about him. Keith died three years before my birth. At three days old, a brain hemorrhage took his life. Since my Mom seldom shared personal emotions, I listened closely to every word. I'll always remember the things she said.

She told me burying Keith was much more difficult than losing Dad. My logic struggled to comprehend. Dad and Mom spent almost fifty years together. Her infant son died 33 years ago. The grief Mom felt for Dad was painful and fresh, but the age-old yearning for her son surpassed it.

"Healing is allowing joy to enter a heart of pain," God explained.

I didn't yet understand, but obviously, the pain of losing a child never, ever leaves a mother-heart!

Mom's next words stunned me. She said, "Your birth puzzled me. When I held you in my arms, I asked God why he took one baby away, just to give me another one." This rare moment of transparency with my mother rocked me. Realization dawned like the morning sun.

God placed me here on this earth. On purpose. I am His idea.

The responsibility of it scared me. A mantle settled onto my shoulders. Deep questions rose within my soul.

Why me? Why do you want me here?

The memory sobered me. Not only did God choose me to be born, but He chose me to survive an accident where I should have died. My Creator showed me a partial answer to the "Why do you want me here?" question. He gave me an assignment, and an audience I didn't seek. I needed to know what to tell them.

So I began to barrage God with my questions.

How do we live with this kind of pain? Is there healing for a wounded heart? You are a Healer. What does that mean for pain of the heart? When someone breaks an arm, it's healed when there is no more pain. When someone has surgery, they know they are healed when there's no more pain. What is healing of the heart? How can we be healed if the pain never ceases? Or is there no healing for this? God, if you want me to talk to people, I need the answers!

I prayed; I read the Scriptures; I read books people gave me about grief; I read autobiographies of loss; I read Christian fictional stories of people who endured pain. Everywhere I searched for nuggets of truth: people, books, God, and the Bible. Answers evaded me for quite some time.

Little by little God revealed the truth. An idea began to form from various pieces of those sources mixed together, until one day a phrase crystallized in my mind.

Healing is not the absence of pain.

Disappointed tears fell down my cheeks. *Then what is healing, God?*

"Healing is allowing joy to enter a heart of pain," God explained.

Oh!! Pain and joy coexisting. That means my heart is functioning again!

Now it made sense. Sometimes memories bring joy and sometimes they bring sadness. It's okay to cry. Don't pretend it doesn't hurt. And it's okay to laugh. The past may bring a smile, or present situations with old and new friends can add memories to my life. Don't stifle the joy either.

In fact, I've learned I *must* express both joy *and* pain. When I avoid one or the other, I lose them both. The concept took a while to process. When I try to eliminate pain in my life, I find I don't experience joy either. It's comparable to a pendulum swinging back and forth in perpetual motion. If I stick an object into the swing of it, to stop it from swinging too far one way, it will also stop swinging as far the other way too. Likewise, the more I deny myself sorrow, the less capable I am of joy.

It's simple, really. A healed heart works again. It's able to feel both positive and negative emotions. Joy and sorrow.

Honestly, I both love and hate the idea.

I love to allow joy into my life and feel it again. My heart celebrates all the memories, good and bad, and cherishes each one. I'm grateful to not pretend when I'm sad; I can cry whenever it swells inside me, for as long as it helps. There are no rules about the length of time it's okay to grieve.

Yet, I hate grieving.

It hurts clear to my toes. I put it off if I can. When it's been awhile since I've laughed, I've avoided grieving too long. It's simply the way it works. I can hide my grief well. Sometimes the pain lies well below the surface of the water. It might be hidden to everyone else, but oh, God sees the depths of my hurt. He doesn't let me hide for long.

He brings the tears, so I can laugh again.

SPLASHES OF JOY

Over a year passed since the accident. The time arrived for the church to choose another pastor. Soon, they made their decision and his family prepared to move into the empty parsonage.

Change colored the horizon.

Memories flooded my mind, both from J.'s ministry here, and from our previous churches. Although I met the pastor and his wife in the present, my mind stayed mostly in the past. I absolutely loved being in the ministry with J. We cared for the church family and considered them "our people." My character and gifting naturally fit what people generally expect of a pastor's wife. The position defined part of my identity.

It didn't really matter who preached on the platform. I thought about J. During his favorite hymns, I pictured him standing at his pew on the stage, singing with his eyes closed and with one hand slightly raised. I saw him preaching in my mind's eye, walking from one side of the pulpit to the other, talking to the people. He often tried to entice them to talk to him during the sermon. If no one responded, he walked to the other side and said, "Maybe I can get someone over here to give me an amen?" Everyone chuckled and paid closer attention.

When it's been awhile since I've laughed, I've avoided grieving too long.

A great deal ran through my mind. It didn't worry me to allow someone different to lead the church. I adjusted well to not being "in the know" anymore and trusted those who made the decisions for our church. Since J. went to heaven, a godly, older man taught us the Scriptures until it was time for a new full-time pastor to come.

Instead, I worried about the pond in the backyard of the parsonage.

I treasured the small pond. It had been a dream come true, really. We built it ourselves, together. We loved the sounds of the water bubbling. The kids enjoyed watching the fish. Our dog loved to drink from it. The sound of running water made our backyard peaceful, like a brook in the mountains.

Our deep pond didn't freeze solid during the winter, but it required regular care. Because no one lived in the parsonage for several months, I felt certain no one tended it. I expected it to be full of moss and probably stink if the pump wasn't running. To prevent our pastor and his wife from wrinkling their noses and tearing it out, I planned to restore it for them. I wanted them to see it the way we created it to be. Then maybe they would keep it.

Journal Entry: March 9, 2006

> *"I've wanted to go clean out the pond and set it up for [the new pastor's] use. I think because I wanted J.'s work to be beautiful to them, not slimy and uncared for as it has been. I was afraid the church would make a decision for them and fill it in. I even heard one member say it would make a good flower bed. I can't describe how afraid I am that they'll do that. I realized yesterday the power of this pond for me—it's like having to give away the most treasured gift that J. and I gave each other."*

Sadly, I thought, "What if they still don't want it?" After all, it was their home to do with as they pleased.

Regardless, I recognized I couldn't do the job alone. It cost too much emotionally. I put it off too long and time caught up with me.

With only a few days left to accomplish it, I didn't know who to ask to help me do such a daunting, probably disgusting task.

The ring of my phone interrupted my deliberation. A lady who attended the women's conference at Pittsburg, Kansas, said, "I couldn't get you off my mind during my Bible study this morning. So I decided to call." She asked about my life. We chatted, and I found myself telling her about the pond and what I wanted to do.

She said, "Do you need help?"

I laughed and said, "Well, it's disgusting. It hasn't been touched for almost a year. I don't think it would be much fun."

The image didn't faze her. When she said, "Let's do it today," I stared at the phone. Not only did she willingly drive about forty-five minutes each way to do this, she also owned her own pond, and knew exactly how to restore its beauty. It dumbfounded me.

My heavenly Father provided exactly what I needed in a most unexpected way. Together we bailed out the old water, scrubbed the rocks, and refilled it with fresh water. I left the parsonage feeling full. The sparkling pond honored the memory J. and I made together. My new friend encouraged me with her gift of service. Droplets of water splashed joy on me straight from heaven. The God of the Universe cared about my silly little pond . . . enough to send someone to help me.

God is good. All the time. I love to tell the story.

Part 5

THE DEPTHS OF LONLINESS

Chapter 15
MORE CHANGE

"I am still confident of this:
I will see the goodness of the Lord *in the land of the living."*

PSALM 27:13

I spoke for about a year, mostly across the Midwest. Then the invitations stopped almost as suddenly as they started. Relief flooded me, but then something close to panic threatened to swallow me. Both my mind and my emotions swam in circles.

Journal entry: January 19, 2007

> *"The requests to speak have stopped. And it makes me terribly insecure! I want to still have that ministry—in fact I feel lost without it. Why? I didn't even want it! Maybe because it gave me purpose and deadlines to strive for. Maybe because I'm afraid people will forget if I don't remind them. Maybe because I liked the attention. Maybe because it gave my life meaning.*
>
> *But God said it would be temporary.*
>
> *I'm amazed as I look behind me and see God's hand at work. I have to admit sometimes I was angry*

> *at God this summer. Every time I wanted some time 'off,' and went on a trip just for fun, it ended up with me speaking, or sharing my story. I wanted somehow to escape it but could not. I don't know that I understand, really, what I even want.*
>
> *I want to find 'Lora,' and yet I never ever want to forget 'Mrs. Lora Jones.' I am who I am because of J. and our children. God forbid I would ever let a day go by without thinking of them! But I have felt so empty, so stuck, like there's nothing I can do but forever live in this story. Yet I want nothing else! And I do not want to quit sharing God's word through this story. What am I going to do?!? Help me God!!"*

The year brought both amazing and intensely difficult experiences. Truly, everywhere I went, God opened a door of opportunity. Some of them made me shake my head and smile.

A NEW PURPOSE

Mom and I took a cruise to Alaska to see one of my nephews and his wife who temporarily lived there. On Sunday morning, we attended the church service on the ship. The pastor didn't arrive to lead it. (How does *that* happen with the ship at sea? He was on the boat somewhere!) Mom spoke up and said, "We already have a speaker," and looked at me. With a small, amused grin at my momma, and only a slight sigh, I stood and shared my story.

Other times, I fumed about what God asked me to do.

One summer weekend, my Jones family and I camped at a small lake in Kansas. While we enjoyed a lovely day, we noticed a gathering by the water. Suddenly, emergency vehicles converged at the campground. Shoved forward by the hand of God, I walked to the mother and sat with her while the authorities searched for the body of her son. Why, God? Why do children drown in this world? There's too much pain here!

I don't know why there's so much pain in this world, but I'm convinced of this: If those of us experienced in suffering don't walk with those freshly experiencing it, then who will? There's nothing like being touched by the hand of someone who understands. It's God with skin on.

As I continued to wrestle with God, one thing became clear: God didn't give me the speaking ministry to bless me with purpose. No. My life should show the world God exists. I can declare what God does for me in thousands of ways. Speaking is only one of them.

It didn't matter whether I continued to share my story in a formal way or not. I will always be able to touch the pain of others with an understanding heart. Then, I can tell them about a God who understands.

A NEW JOB

In the spring of 2007, my brother called to wish me a happy birthday. He surprised me by asking, "Has my pastor called you yet?"

Perplexed, I asked, "No, why?"

My brother said his pastor intended to offer me a job on staff at his church. Flabbergasted, I held my breath while my mind spun out of control.

First Baptist, my home church in Liberal, wants me on their ministerial team?

Sure enough, the pastor called. We talked. I asked lots of questions and argued with his answers. He said he wanted a children's minister. I said, "I really don't enjoy working with children in mass quantities."

The church adjusted their plans to include the adult Bible study ministry in the position. I didn't think I could do both.

He said this idea formed several months ago, but he'd waited for God's timing. I couldn't disagree with that. My speaking engagements appeared to be finished.

Over the course of several weeks, the calls kept going back and forth. I pondered and prayed and doubted. He needed full-time. I proposed part-time. He believed in my abilities. I feared I didn't multitask well enough to run the programs. He should get a medal for his patience.

Finally, I stopped debating with him. I traveled to visit some friends who lived in Houston. They took me to the beach at Galveston, the perfect place to pray until I heard from God.

I strolled on the sand by the water and listened for God's voice. Quietly, His words came to me. "What do you want to do?"

Perhaps I didn't hear correctly. What?

Never did I once expect God to give me a choice. Every test question has a right and wrong answer, right? I'm supposed to choose the correct one. In fact, it frightened me to make the wrong decision. God, of course, heard every word running through my mind, and He answered them. He said, "If you are ready to take another step forward, this is a good one, but if you aren't ready, it's okay to stay in Miami. You can choose."

Love from God embraced me in a brand-new way. His love for me didn't depend on me making exactly the right choice. He simply loved me and allowed me to choose for myself. All the other times I felt pressured to move faster than I thought I could, but this time, God let me decide.

Comforted by His love, I felt braver for the moment, at least. And I knew I wanted to take the ministry position in Liberal.

Stepping forward toward life, I accepted the position, and agreed to begin in the fall.

Without realizing the cost.

A NEW HOME

The summer of 2007 filled with activity nearly every week. Eager to spend time with my kids' friends before I moved, I agreed to be a camp sponsor for three different summer church camps. Saying goodbye already seemed impossibly difficult.

Frequent trips to Liberal became necessary to hunt for a home and complete its purchase. Each time over the last two years, when I traveled to Liberal for a visit, I took some kids from Miami with me. This time two of Jayden's friends accompanied me on the trip to choose my next house. The realtor didn't expect my mom and I to bring two teenage boys with us to tour from place to place, but I enjoyed their antics and listened to their opinions of each house. It made the day easier.

I picked a beautiful home, in move-in condition. Built in 1929, the character of the old house spoke to me, with its original hardwood floors and pull cord windows. With a full basement and five bedrooms, it certainly seemed more than necessary, but it felt right to consider purchasing it.

But what would I do with all the rooms?

God whispered, "Prepare them to be used."

In Miami, my extra bedroom nearly always housed a teenager. Usually a college student rented a room while they attended school. Except for the first few months in the parsonage, I never lived alone. I figured I'd find roommates in Liberal too. Or maybe God might even bring me a second family.

I decided to do some remodeling before I moved into it and hired a carpenter. He removed a wall between two small bedrooms and made it into a large bedroom with a walk-in closet. With those changes, the upstairs became my main home, with a bedroom, bath, and office alongside the living room and kitchen. The basement contained a family room, three more bedrooms, and a large storage room for those precious things I carefully boxed and labeled from the parsonage.

While I enjoyed summer camps, my new home in Liberal transformed. The carpenter modified my bedroom, and some of my precious new church family added fresh paint. In the meantime, I put my home in Miami on the market to sell.

In the past, every time J. and I moved from one church to another and sold our home, it sold quickly. True to the norm, my house went under contract in a few days.

So, when the deal fell through, it shocked me.

The following week, I traveled to Liberal to take care of a few more details on my house. At the same time, a huge storm brought a massive flood to Miami. Most of the town sustained extensive damage. Some homes and businesses were completely destroyed. Many of my friends faced damage, but one family's house wasn't livable. On the other hand, my place sat on higher ground on the edge of town. I received absolutely no damage. The answer dawned on me. I didn't need my house anymore. God did.

I moved to Liberal, leaving my friends in my home. They began to rebuild theirs, and we left my house on the market. As soon as they completed enough work to move into their own home, I received an offer to buy my house. It worked like clockwork. Well, God-work.

THE SAME LONELY PAIN

If I had known in advance how difficult moving away from Miami would be, I wouldn't have gone.

The loneliness for the daily reminders of my children made my heart throb with pain. I missed my children's friends and the stories they shared. I missed my church family's tender care, and their laughter when they retold "J-isms." I missed the companionship around the table while the college students studied. I even missed being known as "that lady who lost her family."

Once again, I fell into my old habits. I didn't express my emotions honestly because it might hurt people I loved.

Now I lived in a community that saw me as the girl who grew up here. Suddenly back in the world of my childhood, I was only Lora. But who was she, and did I want to be her?

I refrained from saying any of this to my family who lived in Liberal. They welcomed me home with excitement. It didn't feel fair to be homesick when I lived in my hometown. Once again, I fell into my old habits. I didn't express my emotions honestly because it might hurt people I loved. But, covering my feelings caused me to draw inward.

Journal Entry: December 31, 2007

"Waking up to my alarm of Midsummer Night's Dream, it sounded so much like a wedding I wanted to throw it, or hide, or stay in bed forever. That's when I realized hope is what I'm missing. Hope. I've lost hope.

Yesterday's sermon was about the song of Mary, the mother of Jesus. The speaker asked, 'What song will you sing in 2008?' He said, 'Once you've heard the song of God, you will never be the same.' I know that. I asked the pastor to pray for me. I've lost my song."

To distract myself, I focused on my new position. The job required remembering lots of details and multitasking. Since I struggled with both, I concentrated on learning as much as possible about the programs of the church.

The church used a children's program called AWANA [Approved Workmen Are Not Ashamed] that was entirely new to me. When I discovered a training event for the program in Garden City, Kansas, I registered to go with two other ladies I'd never met.

One of them appeared at my house the week before the conference, bringing me breakfast from Sonic. I found out later Brenda didn't like the idea of traveling with a stranger, so she decided to meet me first.

God had other ideas.

The woman saw with God's eyes. He gave her the gift of mercy, enabling her to see the pain others often miss. Therefore, when I opened the door, she saw me. I mean she truly saw *me*, not the person I tried overly hard to be. I pretended to be happy to be home, and excited about the job. The truth showed in my eyes—terrible loneliness, deep pain and fear. She saw it all.

Sometimes God tells on me without my permission.

Sometimes God tells on me without my permission.

Brenda didn't say a word, but she thought, "Whoever that lady is, she needs help."

She knew nothing of my story, or my background in Liberal. I'd grown up with her husband, but neither of us realized it yet. She didn't know I took a ministry position at her church. But she knew my pain ran deep, and she intended to help.

God seemed far away and quiet to me, but He actively worked on my behalf. He sent me someone I needed, even though I didn't recognize it yet—someone who saw through my pretense.

I don't know why I pretended to be okay. From the beginning, I committed to grieve openly and transparently. Maybe I figured I should be capable of living by now. Maybe I assumed others expected me to be independent by now. Maybe there's not a reasonable explanation.

The rays of hope dropped behind a cloud of loneliness.

I'd lost my song.

Chapter 16

HIDDEN ANGER

". . . If a man owns a hundred sheep, and one of them wanders away, will he not leave the ninety-nine on the hills and go to look for the one that wandered off?"

MATTHEW 18:12

When God spoke again, His words came from a very unexpected source.

One day, Brenda came to visit me. With concern etched on her face, she exhaled audibly, then told me a story.

It started as a typical night at their house. Brenda and her seven-year-old daughter, Brianna, chatted in their carefree, usual way. But the conversation turned serious when Brianna asked about my family. Her momma tenderly explained what happened to them. She responded, "Wow. Did she say thank you?"

Brenda stopped and stared at me. I blinked and cocked my head to one side, perplexed. Why did Brianna think I should be thankful for this situation in my life? Shaking the question away, I decided I honestly didn't care to know what she thought. So I changed the subject.

That night, my friend let me avoid the issue, but a few days later, she came by my house again. This time she told me I needed to deal with her daughter's words. Looking straight into my eyes, she said, "Brianna asked again if you said thank you. When I tried to explain to her how difficult it is for you, Brianna shook her head and said, 'God must be so sad.'"

"What in the world is she thinking?!" My voice began to rise, and then I softened. I reminded myself we were talking about a child—her child. "Why does she want me to be thankful for the accident?"

"That's not what she meant," Brenda gently responded.

"What does she mean?!" The frustration built within me.

"She wants to know if you are thankful to be alive," Brenda answered.

Something absolutely exploded inside of me. The dam holding my pain burst. "NOOOO, I am NOT thankful to be alive!" Bitter tears began to fall, but no comfort came with them.

Journal Entry: January 7, 2008

> *"I can be thankful for many things—that God has my children, they are safe, that I got to have them, for J. and his love, for the many who love me, for Miami, for the incredible growth in my faith with the Lord, for His presence, His love, His comfort, His promises . . . but not for the accident.*
>
> *I told Brenda all these things last night. She gently responded, 'That's not what she meant. She wants to know if you are thankful to be alive.'*
>
> *Well, perhaps that's even harder. I've always said they got the better end of the deal. I've said I'll take the assignment, be faithful, tell the story—but be thankful for life? I must admit, I'm stuck on that one.*
>
> *Then I got a text from Brenda that she and Bri are praying for me. How can I fight against a 7-year-old's prayers? Aargh.*

> *Each time I awoke last night, a song phrase kept coming to me. 'I go to the desert to find my sheep.'[80] I know I am in a desert, but I don't want to be found."*

The week ahead brought many explosions of anger and tears. Unexperienced with this side of grieving, even though three years had passed since the accident, the hot anger blindsided me. Deeply hidden within me festered my death wish. The questions I'd settled resurfaced.

Deeply hidden within me festered my death wish.

Why didn't I get to go with them? Have I done enough yet to be finished here? How can life be good without them?

Days went by and Brenda continued to challenge me. I knew I must get on my face before God, but I felt no desire to talk to Him.

Finally, I spewed angry but honest words at Him.

I don't want to be thankful; I really don't like this life at all. Why did you leave me here?

Throughout the day, I noticed my rage began to slightly lessen.

EMBRACING LIFE

The next day I sat at my office desk attempting to focus when a lady came in to talk to me. With a pill bottle in her hand, I easily recognized the suicidal battle raging in her mind. Urgently, I tried to convince her to live for her children.

"God has a plan for your life," I said. "You matter to Him. And you matter to your children."

My own anger boiled within me. *You. Have. Children. How can you consider taking yourself away from them on purpose? It's so cruel to them. Besides, how is that not enough for you to want to live? I long for the life you have, and you don't even want it!*

Some of those words may have been audible because suddenly, she stopped arguing with me and said, "What are you going to do?"

Stunned, I began to pray aloud for her in an attempt to refocus myself. Instead, God drove the point home during the prayer, and I found myself praying for the desire to live. When I finished praying and looked up, the lady's face radiated peace. Her turmoil completely gone, she simply stood and left my office.

I walked straight into my pastor's office and told him the whole story—from Brenda coming to talk to me about Brianna's words, to the suicidal lady in my office. He leaned back in his chair and said words I'll never forget. "God has just shown you a mirror."

Realization sunk to my toes. The exposure of my sin felt like a thief caught in the light of the policeman's spotlight. My pastor was right. I didn't try to take my life, but I lived with the same despondency. For me to hate the gift of life God gave me equaled the sin of suicide in His eyes. Brianna was right.

God *was* sad.

Retreating home, I fell to my knees on my bedroom floor. I poured out my anger and sadness. In repentance, I agreed with God about how much I hurt Him by not wanting this plan He created for me. Next, I simply *chose* to be obedient. With a heavy heart, I prayed, "I choose to say thank you for life. It's all I've got. Work with it."

I didn't *feel* thankful yet, but I offered the honest attempt to try. Day after day I knelt and thanked God for life without emotion. In time, my attitude softened toward God and my prayers became humbler.

Journal Entry: January 15, 2008

> *"O Holy Creator, I have no right to look into your face. I have sinned against you. Help me desire to live . . . to long to see your face . . . but not long to die. Help me have joy in this life . . . to be thankful for the gift. Wash my heart clean. Please continue to tender my heart to recognize sin."*

In 1868, Elizabeth Clephane wrote the song God sang to me the night Brianna first asked her question. I remembered it from childhood when Mom and Dad played their old Tennessee Ernie Ford albums. What a beautiful story it tells of the love of our tender Shepherd, who will go to the desert to find His sheep.

There were ninety and nine that safely lay
In the shelter of the fold;
But one was out on the hills away,
Far off from the gates of gold.
Away on the mountains wild and bare;
Away from the tender Shepherd's care;
Away from the tender Shepherd's care.

"Lord, Thou hast here Thy ninety and nine;
Are they not enough for Thee?"
But the Shepherd made answer: "This of Mine
Has wandered away from Me.
And although the road be rough and steep,
I go to the desert to find My sheep;
I go to the desert to find My sheep."

But none of the ransomed ever knew
How deep were the waters crossed;
Nor how dark was the night the Lord passed through
Ere He found His sheep that was lost.
Out in the desert He heard its cry;
'Twas sick and helpless and ready to die;
'Twas sick and helpless and ready to die.

"Lord, whence are those blood-drops all the way,
That mark out the mountain's track?"
"They were shed for one who had gone astray
Ere the Shepherd could bring him back."
"Lord, whence are Thy hands so rent and torn?"
"They're pierced tonight by many a thorn;
They're pierced tonight by many a thorn."

But all through the mountains, thunder-riv'n,
And up from the rocky steep,
There arose a glad cry to the gate of heav'n,
"Rejoice! I have found My sheep!"

And the angels echoed around the throne,
"Rejoice, for the Lord brings back His own!
Rejoice, for the Lord brings back His own."[81]

All of heaven rejoiced when I willingly returned to the fold.

God sent Jesus, so I can join my family in heaven someday and live eternally. That's truth. There's another truth, however. God gave me *this* life *too*. It continues to challenge me to have the faith of my daughter to cry out, "The only reason I'm alive today is because of Jesus."

It's time to wrap myself in the joy of living.

THE DESIRE OF MY HEART

With new determination to find joy in the present instead of only in the past, I threw myself into my work at the church. Over the next three years, I enjoyed watching people in the small groups and Bible studies. I loved to see them understand something about God's character for the first time.

Occasionally, I still received the opportunity to share my story at a women's retreat or a Bible study group. Each time I sensed the presence of God in a powerful way. I looked forward to these events. They refilled my energy to serve the Lord. It amazed me to observe God speak into the lives of others through my story. I found myself wishing to return to the year I spoke full-time.

Amused with myself, I remembered how I fought against God when He asked me to speak. Now, I wanted to do it again. Fickle woman. My present ministry kept me too busy to allow myself to be distracted by the dream. Besides, I reasoned, it couldn't possibly be *God's* plan—because *I* wanted it. He usually asked difficult things. I told myself to get back to work.

What's the desire of my heart for today?

One day, as I read the Bible, I came across a familiar verse in Psalm 37:4. "Delight yourself in the LORD and he will give you the desires of your heart." I stopped and pondered this a few minutes.

What is the desire of my heart? To see my husband and children again, for sure, but that's the distant future. What's the desire of my heart for today? To have the freedom to travel and speak again, without the constraints of a second job.

I gasped aloud when the light bulb came on.

God gave me this desire. He asked me to speak, and I did—reluctantly, but obediently. When the season ended, He gave me a ministry job. During those three years, I began to yearn to do what God asked me to do in the first place. His plan worked. He spoon-fed me at first, so my taste buds learned to crave it. This desire came from God.

I'm free to go.

The church didn't see it coming. I stunned them when I quit, but when I explained, they understood and gladly supported my return to the speaking ministry.

Excitement filled my face—very different from the first time I answered the call to speak. With a light heart and a sense of anticipation, I left my office for the last time.

I embraced the joy of the present, finally thankful for life.

Part 6

GIFTS OF HOPE

Chapter 17

MY KIDS

". . . You anoint my head with oil; my cup overflows. Surely goodness and love will follow me all the days of my life, and I will dwell in the house of the Lord forever."

PSALM 23:5-6

Joy comes in a variety of ways, but nothing brings more than children. A wealth of memories from the fourteen years I enjoyed being a mom prove it. At first, the recollections of my children brought aching pain. I only thought about how much I yearned to make more of them. Eventually, however, those same stories became priceless joy to me. Today, precious glimpses into the past often bring a smile to my lips while I pause to remember. Those who know me best recognize the far-off look I get in my eyes when I disappear into a memory.

THE JOY OF CHILDREN

Walking through the grocery store seeing a small boy with his mother can remind me of a particular trip to the grocery store with my little ones in tow. At four years old, Jayden claimed a multitude of imaginary brothers, all of whom he called "John-John." One day I pushed my cart through the store while studying my grocery list. Suddenly, Jayden threw himself violently to the floor.

He laid there, sprawled on the tile in the middle of the aisle, and proclaimed, "Did you see that? John-John just pushed me down!"

Oh my. Embarrassed, I gritted my teeth together, and quietly growled, "Get. Up. Jayden."

Now when I think of it, I giggle. So, if you ever see me walking through the canned goods aisle giggling, staring at the floor, you will know my secret.

Unlikely things bring a flood of memories. Masking tape reminds me of the day Janessa taped across the bathroom doorway while Jayden took a shower. When he opened the door in his towel, she stood in the hallway, ready with a camera. He stood there staring at the spider's web of tape blocking his exit. Her laughter rang out until the tears streamed down her cheeks.

Sometimes something triggers the memory, but often it randomly appears. Occasionally I want to share the thoughts, but mostly I keep them quietly to myself, treasuring them deep within my heart.

The joy of being a mother has no bounds, but the depth of pain from living without them is bottomless. My love for them did not diminish over time. No. It intensified. I cannot wait to see them again. Running straight into their arms, I will hold on and not let go until their laughter beckons me to run with them down the streets of gold.

BEING CALLED MOM

By 2010, my mom said I had more children than anyone she's met. She's right. I'm blessed, although it took me a long time to recognize it. How did it come to be?

A few extra kids called me Mom when my own children were still on this earth. They spent a lot of time at our house playing with my children, and it seemed natural to them to call me Mom. I considered it an honor.

Following the accident, those kids continued to call me Mom. It meant the world to me. Those special few, I still call mine today. I celebrated with them during graduations from middle school, high school, college, and basic training, and now weddings and babies. It's amazed me to be given a special role in those festivities. They mean so much to me. I believe in them and encourage them while they start their families and dream of grand careers.

To be called "Mom" is a gift of the highest honor.

Another group of kids from my children's friends didn't call me Mom, but they include me in their world, nevertheless.

Some are childhood friends of Janessa's from Grand Island, her little-girl friends from age two to nine. Together they made me a scrapbook of their favorite memories with Janessa. I will treasure it forever. They still call or message me from time to time to check on me or catch me up on their world.

I'll never forget their first year of college. During spring break, two of them road-tripped to Liberal to visit me. I'm amazed by parents willing to share their children with me. We enjoyed a wonderful time together, remembering the past and sharing stories of the present.

More of my "kids" come from Miami. They attended grade school and middle school with Jayden and Janessa. Many of them contact me on Facebook, or simply text me when there's something on their mind. It's amazing to watch them grow into adulthood, and gratifying to see their faith grow. When they call to tell me a God-story in their lives, I dance around the room.

Occasionally I'm surprised to hear from someone new—most recently a couple of young men from Jayden's childhood soccer team. Tears of gratitude rolled down my face. My children are not forgotten.

When Janessa turned twenty-five, I decided to do something special. I planned a trip to visit her friends. For ten days, I traveled from one to another—1,600 miles, four states, and sixteen girls—the trip of a lifetime, though I hope someday to repeat it. I loved every girl, every moment, and every smile. Each young woman with a unique story, but one thing in common. Janessa. Her witness continues to influence lives. This momma couldn't be prouder.

I honestly thought I was incapable of truly loving anyone again, especially a child. Love risks losing again.

There's also the group of college students from 2005 and 2006. That's another extensive list of graduations, weddings, and babies! Several of those kids call me Mom (or Ma) too. They naturally assigned me the honorary title when they spent a great deal of time at my house, washed their clothes there, and ate meals with me. Some of them surprised me by continuing the term after I moved to Liberal, and they moved away from Miami.

So, often my siblings ask me where I'm going, and I simply say, "To see one of my kids." I do my best to attend everything because it matters to me. They matter to me. Although sometimes I feel like the old woman who lived in a shoe.

There isn't any way for anyone to ease the lonely ache in me for Janessa and Jayden, but these kids do two things for me: First, when they tell a story about my children, it proves they aren't forgotten. Nothing could be more important to me. Second, they keep my Momma-heart alive. In other words, they let me "mother" them. I honestly thought I was incapable of truly loving anyone again, especially a child. Love risks losing again. Too scary. Over the years, inch by inch, these kids tempted me to take the risk, in ways I never saw coming.

THE RISK OF LOVING

At some point along the way, I began to wonder what it would be like to marry again and become a stepmother. From my perspective, I questioned my capability to love another child with the same depth of love I shared with my own children. And if I succeeded, they might not love me in return—the loss equally difficult for them.

Journal Entry: June 14, 2012

> *"I imagine someday marrying again, to be a mom again. I imagine what it would be like to take another child, to learn to love again. But what I want the very most: to be loved in return. The day when I know that the child has accepted me into their world and loves me as a mom. Oh, how my heart aches for that."*

God never does anything the way I expect He will.

Will continued to call me Mom after we both left Miami. Known to his friends as "Mountain Man," he lives to climb. During his time in college, he always called me before one of his adventures—mostly since he enjoyed making me worry a bit. I earned the right to be concerned the day I met him at the ER for stitches. That's when his mom and I bonded. She was too far away to come to the hospital. It meant a lot to her for me to be there.

Her diagnosis caught me by surprise. Cancer. We walked through the lengthy, tearful journey together. Although we prayed for healing on this earth, God chose to heal her by giving her eternal life in heaven.

Now, it means something different to Will when he calls me Mom. We still talk about his mom, celebrating special memories of her. I hear from him all the time—when bears go through his tent or when he's "hanging around" on the climbing wall. He makes me smile . . . and worry a little bit. It's what moms do, right?

Adam began to call me Mom because he loved to ask for my opinion, and then have a good argument about my advice! He delighted in stirring up some controversial discussion around my kitchen table in Miami. Adam and his parents enjoy a close relationship, but for some reason, he continued to call me Mom for several years. God's plan took a while to reveal itself.

This story begins with another college student. I met Teresa when Adam brought her to my house one day for dinner. Their relationship didn't last very long, but I continued to interact with Teresa through the Baptist Collegiate Ministry at NEO (Northeastern Oklahoma A&M College in Miami).

When I moved to Liberal and took the job at First Baptist, the church agreed to hire a summer intern for me. Naturally, I wrote to my kids from NEO to inquire if any of them wanted to come. Teresa responded. She came to live and work with me for the summer of 2008. We became such a good team, she returned two more summers. During this time, she began to feel a calling of her own to the children's ministry.

Much happened in Teresa's life during this time of ministry-calling. Her mother began to struggle with her health, and then, unexpectedly, died. Again, I found myself walking a journey of grief with one of "my kids." It's extremely hard for a young adult to lose a parent. In a time of life when they try to stretch their wings and fly without their parent's aid, they still need their mom and dad. Their parents become the touchstone which keeps them grounded while they try to soar on their own.

For Teresa, life became even more difficult when her father received a dreaded diagnosis. Cancer. When she graduated from John Brown University in December 2011, his failing health prevented his chance to celebrate with her. Surrounded by her brother's family and me, she said good-bye to college life and considered the next part of her life's journey.

About the same time, our church in Liberal invited a new pastor to lead the church. He began to seek a staff member specifically for children. Teresa wrestled with the decision to move far away from her father. She wanted to be nearby to help take care of him. He hoped she followed her calling and found a place to serve the Lord. His tender words encouraged her to try it. She applied.

We celebrated when she received the Children's Ministry position. Soon, she moved in with me again, ready to begin her dream come true. Her father beamed with pride.

Within Teresa's first month in Liberal, her daddy suffered a stroke. Expecting the worst, she struggled to face what appeared to be inevitable. Back and forth she traveled, spending every available day off with him.

God graciously gave them more time than any of us dreamed.

In the midst of the turmoil, Adam and Teresa began to date again. Throughout the years, they remained friends and communicated from time to time. Adam moved to Liberal to facilitate spending more time together, and their relationship quickly became serious. They surprised me when they announced their engagement.

Time seemed to be of the essence. We began to pray Teresa's father would live to see them wed.

My role with Teresa continued to deepen. Living together throughout her heartache opened the door to a relationship neither of us really expected. Gradually, God challenged us both to accept each other as family. Teresa asked me one day to be her "Mom" at the wedding. Stunned, I focused on her face. Right in front of me, I saw a child looking at me with eyes of love. I didn't see it coming.

Journal Entry: July 23, 2012

"Father, I stand in awe of you. What a gift. It's still sinking in.

It was a couple of weeks ago that Teresa asked me to take the mom role in her wedding. I was stunned. Wow. I wrote about the desire for a child in my journal barely six weeks ago. I wanted to tell her what I had written, but no words would come out of my mouth. I just handed it to her and let her read it.

I'm just astounded. But it is taking me awhile to grasp it. I realized right away that receiving the gift is hard. It requires putting down a gate of my heart, and allowing it to love in a way I haven't been capable of loving for the last nearly 8 years. It requires taking a risk. It requires taking responsibility. It requires long term commitment. It requires traveling to see them, meeting their needs, praying for them, Christmases, holidays, birthdays, everything . . . even grandchildren. And it even requires dealing with some guilt because I want so badly to have been able to do these things with Janessa instead.

Who would've ever thought you would do this in this order Father? To grant me a child. A child. Not a stepchild. A child."

Five months later, I walked down the aisle as the mother of the bride. Suddenly, I gained a son-in-law who had already been calling me Mom for the last seven years. It makes me smile how God planned it well before I even considered loving another child like my own.

Words can't express the emotions roiling through my soul on her wedding day. The wrestling within me was deep and painful. I wanted to celebrate with Teresa, and I knew she needed me to rejoice with her. But I longed to celebrate this day with Janessa, even though I can't.

Specific details of the wedding day twisted the knife in my heart. Adam attended our church in Miami, and volunteered with the youth, therefore many of those present would have been on Janessa's wedding guest list. Tyson, her youth pastor, helped perform the ceremony. Teresa and Adam chose their venue to be Grand Lake Baptist Assembly Campgrounds, where my children went to camp. My kids' friends attended the wedding. In fact, the young man who escorted me down the aisle calls me Mom from those precious days of playing with my son at our house.

The past and the present mixed together with the flashbacks vivid enough to affect my ability to concentrate. I couldn't focus, nor think clearly. It embarrassed me how much I forgot to do. Someone drove thirty miles to retrieve Teresa's shoes since I left them in the motel room. I became simply a robot trying to survive.

Just because it's hard doesn't mean it isn't right and good.

Sometimes in life I wish do-overs existed. But I can't fathom how to do it over and get through it any better.

Yes, I'd do it again. Just because it's hard doesn't mean it isn't right and good.

Teresa comforted me through the years when she knew I struggled with grief. Her gentle personality naturally brings peace to turmoil. Then life dealt a cruel blow, and she experienced loss first hand. On her wedding day, she beamed with excitement, but she also fought her own battle with loneliness. Her momma should have been there.

Pulling me aside, she asked, "How ya doing?" The question opened the floodgate of tears I tried desperately to hide. Her grief found release too, and we cried together—a momma missing her daughter, and a child missing her momma.

Lovingly, God answered our prayers for Teresa's Dad. Abandoning the wheelchair, he proudly walked her down the aisle. He and I sat side by side, connected together only by our love for the beautiful girl dressed in white.

God blessed Teresa with another year of life for her daddy before he joined his wife for the celebration in heaven.

Opening my heart to risk love challenges every fiber of my being. When the accident happened, something within me shut down. Not my faith. My capacity to love. Wrapped in fear of loss, I balked at loving again. Yet, some special people in my life make it possible to risk love. Teresa is one of those. She's the daughter I share with her two amazing parents in heaven.

Finally, I realized what God had been doing for years. He hammered at the wall around my heart with every child who called me Mom. With every young adult who loved me, God chipped away at my well-built defenses. Teresa's story helped break a hole in the wall which allowed me to love *all* my kids more deeply. They deserved more than I gave—until now.

RUTH AND NAOMI

There's a story in the Bible about a woman who lost her entire family. Naomi and her husband lived in Israel and raised two sons. When a severe famine plagued their land, they chose to move to Moab to find food. While living there, Naomi's husband and both sons died.

I identify with Naomi.

Lost and empty, Naomi decided to move back to her country. She asked nothing of her Moabite daughters-in-law. Instead she urged them to return to their families and start new lives.

One of them did, but the other refused to leave. Ruth said, ". . . Don't urge me to leave you or to turn back from you. Where you go I will go, and where you stay I will stay. Your people will be my people and your God my God. Where you die I will die, and there I will be buried . . ." (Ruth 1:16-17).

Teresa is my Ruth.

Naomi stopped protesting, but she didn't absorb the implications of Ruth's offer. When they arrived in Israel, she asked her former friends to call her Mara, meaning bitter, instead of Naomi, which translates to pleasant. "I went away full, but the LORD has brought me back empty. Why call me Naomi? The LORD has afflicted me . . ." (Ruth 1:21).

It took her awhile to realize she wasn't alone.

God gave Naomi a lifetime gift in Ruth. She left her own country to go with her mother-in-law to her homeland. There Ruth married Boaz. Together they took care of Naomi until the day she died. They brought joy to her life again, and laid grandchildren in her lap. Finally, the wall of bitterness in Naomi's heart crumbled.[82]

Teresa identifies with Ruth. She didn't lose her husband, but she lost both parents and chose to commit herself to a lady who felt left behind. One day, Adam came to me with this Bible story and said, "I realize now, I'm Boaz. You are my responsibility. I'm young, and I don't know a lot, or have much, but I'll take care of you."

The final walls of my defenses crumbled at my feet.

I left home a young woman full of hope and plans for a future. Those plans unfolded beautifully with J., Janessa, and Jayden, but I returned with empty hands. Until God filled my life again with adult children who chose to love me.

You and me, me and you
Where you go, I'll go too
I'm with you. I'm with you . . .[83]

Nichole Nordeman and Amy Grant sing a duet called "I'm With You (Ruth & Naomi)."[84] In the song, Naomi and Ruth tell the story of their lives. Teresa and I adopted the song for ourselves.

The final refrain speaks my message for "my kids."

Who can say I'm left with nothing
When I have all of you, all of you?
In the way you always love me
I remember He does too.[85]

Chapter 18

SOARING ABOVE THE STORM

". . . those who hope in the Lord *will renew their strength. They will soar on wings like eagles; they will run and not grow weary, they will walk and not be faint."*

ISAIAH 40:31

Right in the middle of teaching me how to embrace joy and love, God also taught me to continue to grieve.

One day, weary and dull, I struggled with the motivation to accomplish anything. My mind tried to think of too many things at once. I sat down in my favorite chair and began to pray for peace, until the old hymn "Be Still, My Soul"[86] came to mind. I only remembered a few of the words, so I googled them. Singing as I read them, these words caught my attention:

Be still my soul! the Lord is on thy side;
Bear patiently the cross of grief or pain;
Leave to thy God to order and provide;
In every change He faithful will remain.
Be still, my soul! thy best, thy heavenly Friend
Thro' thorny ways leads to a joyful end.[87]

CROSS OF GRIEF

What is the "cross of grief or pain?"[88] I pondered the question for several days and asked the Lord what it meant. The Bible says in Matthew 16:24, "Then Jesus said to his disciples, 'If anyone would come after me, he must deny himself and take up his cross and follow me.'" To me, taking up your cross had meant being willing to die for your belief in Jesus. He, after all, died on a cross for me.

The song didn't say the cross of death, however. It said the cross of grief or pain. What did the songwriter mean? God soon answered the question in bold color.

In the spring of 2012, I read an e-mail advertisement about an upcoming trip to Brazil. I didn't expect to ever return to South America, but the trip lingered in my thoughts. When I prayed about it, God urged me to go. Not understanding why, I signed up, paid my deposit, and began to plan for an international mission trip.

Just a few weeks before time to leave, I received a message concerning a young couple from the Brazil Pioneer Missions building team. In today's world, messages sometimes cross miles almost too quickly. This prayer alert said an auto accident occurred. The couple's children died, but they hadn't been told yet. We didn't know the condition of the father, but the mother was being transported to the hospital where her husband had already been admitted.

I froze.

Seriously, God? This is why I'm supposed to go to Brazil?

Angry, frightened tears streamed down my face. The bile of bitterness long swallowed regurgitated into my mouth and tasted nasty.

I don't want to do this. I can't relive those first weeks. Please don't make me.

Shame washed over me, but it didn't change the pity-party. I should have been crying for them, not for myself!

Thus began a debate in my mind with the old song. Is this what it meant to carry the cross of grief and pain? I certainly didn't want to "bear patiently" *that* cross. It simply hurt too much.

Journal Entry: April 5, 2012

"I know I have not considered grief as a cross because I still desperately want to believe there is an end to pain in people's lives and hearts on earth . . . a point in time where the event no longer brings pain. I know it doesn't happen. Yet, it doesn't contradict the many verses that talk about joy, or life to the full . . . both exist . . . in the same person, at the same time. I just don't want to hurt . . . and I don't want my loved ones to hurt . . . ever. There will be a time when all sorrow will end and joy will be complete, uninterrupted, unchallenged, undefiled, pure, everlasting joy . . . when we see Him face to face. We get only moments of joy now . . . when we are still . . . when our soul is still . . ."

Be still, my soul! thy God doth undertake
To guide the future, as He has the past.
Thy hope, thy confidence let nothing shake;
All now mysterious shall be bright at last.
Be still, my soul! the waves and winds still know
His voice who ruled them while He dwelt below.[89]

"Quiet! Be still!" Jesus said to the waves when the disciples were afraid. The waves immediately became still . . ."[90] *The same is true of the waves of my soul. That perhaps, more than anything, is why I need my "quiet time" . . . so for a moment, the waves can be calm . . ."*

It's a hard thing to walk the middle ground of embracing both joy and pain. This time, however, I needed to do it for someone else. Walking into their pain required me to allow myself to feel my own initial pain again. That's why it made me angry about what I would have to do in Brazil. I didn't want to delve back into those days of excruciating heartache.

A wrestling match began between my love for them and my own selfishness.

Within a few days, I heard from the team leader. He said what we both knew. "This is why you are supposed to go to Brazil this year."

I agreed, but asked him to pray for me, and then together we prayed for this sweet couple, their injured bodies, and their broken hearts.

Expert Brazilian bricklayers, they built walls with precision and speed. J. and I had seen them work together on my first trip. There seemed to be an attraction between them, and we wondered if they might someday become a team. Sure enough, in a year or two, they married. Soon thereafter, they started a family. At the point of their accident, two little girls filled their home with joy.

Both parents survived the accident, but we certainly didn't expect them to be at work on the team when we arrived in Brazil a few short weeks later. Instead, the team leader prepared a way for me to go to them.

I began to consider what to say to them. When I pondered through everything people said to me in the early weeks, nothing came to mind which made a difference. Their presence, not their words, mattered. Remembering this helped since I couldn't speak their language without an interpreter anyway. I simply asked the Lord to help me be honest with them emotionally.

In no time at all, I headed to Brazil. To my surprise, the couple met our bus. I easily wrapped my arms around them and held them quietly. They recognized me—they knew J. —they remembered our story. Our hearts simply understood each other.

The week went by and mostly I watched them. It was surreal, seeing my own past through them. I saw the strength of God clearly on their faces, exactly like people described to me in 2004. Someone said, "They are so strong," and I added, "What we see is God's strength in their weakness."

Unable to physically work, the young man talked to people about Jesus, and told his own story. Several people responded to the message and believed in God's love for the first time. Clearly, God urged this man of faith to teach others about Him. It reminded me of how God

Facing my own grief and allowing it to surface enabled my heart to function properly again.

confirmed his calling within me when He told me to start sharing my story.

In the meantime, a local Brazilian church asked me to speak for their worship service with an interpreter. I spoke, but I felt disconnected from the presence of God and struggled with what to say.

The next day, I talked with one of my team members about it, and he suggested I rest awhile before volunteering at the vision center. So, when I got off the bus, I sat outside the mission building on the concrete to simply be still and rest. Suddenly, grief blindsided me. Usually, something either comes to mind or triggers my emotions, but this time, it hit me out of nowhere. When I abruptly started sobbing, I began to pray, "God, please, please help me stop."

But I couldn't stop.

Quietly God said, "You asked to be real."

Well, yes, I did.

The pain intensified, both emotionally and physically. People gathered around and began to pray. Someone began to sing a chorus, until my lips sang along.

You give and take away.
You give and take away.
My heart will choose to say
Lord, blessed be Your name.[91]

I felt better afterward, or maybe I should say I *could* feel after pouring out the pain. When I spoke again the following day, I sensed the presence of the Lord. I don't think He was absent the first time; I simply had been incapable of feeling His Spirit. Facing my own grief and allowing it to surface enabled my heart to function properly again.

God moved among people over the next few days. Although there's no way for me to discern everything God orchestrated for others, I certainly know one of the things He did in me. He challenged me to not fear the pain of carrying a cross of grief. Through this trip, He taught me to be willing to express my pain, so I can fearlessly walk beside someone else in their sorrow. Besides, it makes me real —truthful about my emotions with myself, and with others.

Until someday, when all sorrow fades away . . .

Be still, my soul! the hour is hast'ning on
When we shall be forever with the Lord.
When disappointment, grief, and fear are gone,
Sorrow forgot, love's purest joys restored.
Be still, my soul! when change and tears are past
All safe and blessed we shall meet at last.[92]

EAGLES' WINGS

I often imagine my arrival in heaven. The excitement makes my heart pound with anticipation. Closing my eyes, I let the dream soar above the clouds of doubt and winds of distractions from this physical life. My mind's eye sees me racing across the space in between us into their arms again. The air smells pure, clean, and fresh. Sorrow forgotten. Hope made sight.

These images become the most vivid when I'm outside, away from the hustle and bustle of life. Camping beside a lake, horseback riding on a mountain, or sailing on an ocean give me time and space to dream. Starlit nights, snow-capped mountains, and babbling brooks make me feel closer to my Maker and fill me with hope for the future. I treasure many precious memories from those adventures with God, but none are as tender to me as the unexpected pleasure of watching bald eagles feed in an ocean inlet.

One of the last great sermons J. L. preached included an illustration about eagles. I will never forget the sermon, and I'm not the only one who says so. He presented it at our regular church service in September 2004, and later, shared it again at an associational meeting to a group of pastors. In the sermon, he described how we hold tight to our preferences and traditions. Using himself to illustrate the point, he picked up a church hymnal, placed it under his arm, and said, "I want this kind of music in my church." Then he grabbed his Bible and tucked it under his arm and said, "I want this version of the Bible used in my church." Again, he took a church pew cushion and shoved it under his other arm and said, "I want to sit in this spot each Sunday."

Continuing the pattern until nothing else fit under his arms, he recited Isaiah 40:31: ". . . those who hope in the LORD will renew their strength. They will soar on wings like eagles; they will run and not grow weary, they will walk and not be faint."

Looking down at his collection, he asked, "How are ya gonna fly with all this stuff?" Slowly, he spread out his arms, and everything crashed to the floor. When the noise settled, he told us, "You have to let go of everything in order to fly!"

"Think about the eagle," he continued. "The mother eagle teaches her babies to fly by pushing them out of the nest. She simply shoves them over the side and watches them struggle to fly. Then she swoops under them and catches them on her wing, allowing them to rest—before she flips them back off again to practice some more. If they continually just fly back to the nest, refusing to soar, then she will literally take apart the nest, so they cannot go back to its safety. She seriously wants them to fly!"

"If your world seems to be out of your control and falling apart, is it because of your own choices, or is it because God has taken apart your nest, so you have to fly?"

As he brought the point home, J. asked us to consider this: "If your world seems to be out of your control and falling apart, is it because of your own choices, or is it because God has taken apart your nest, so you have to fly?"

I didn't forget his sermon when my nest came apart.

It made a lasting impression on me.

J.'s headstone is in the shape of a mountain, engraved with an eagle flying toward the sun whose rays peek through the clouds. Beside the eagle are two smaller eagles, also flying toward the sun.

In 2013, I cruised to Alaska again, this time with Brenda and her family. One day, we chose an excursion on a crab boat. With fascination, we listened to the crew describe the process of their trade. They taught us about the crabs and even let us hold some of the smaller ones. The fishermen held the king crabs for us—above our heads for a photo shoot. Yikes.

My mind wandered to this day, twenty-eight years ago—my wedding day. I thought about how much J. would have enjoyed this trip to Alaska, and the crab boat excursion.

The crew master interrupted my reverie on the loud speaker, "We have a surprise for you."

They maneuvered the boat into a cove and said, "Every day we come here to feed the bald eagles." As they tossed shad into the water as far as a human arm can toss, around twenty-five bald eagles swooped down from the sky to snatch the fish from the water. I stood wide-eyed, trying to take in every movement, but tears kept getting in the way of clear sight. Amazed by God's love vividly displayed in front of me, I whispered, "Thank you, Father."

No one on the crew knew of my anniversary. They certainly weren't aware of the significance of eagles to me. God knew. He understood my loneliness for my husband and designed the perfect gift of love to me.

I reflected on the sermon, and let it remind me of his challenge to soar with the eagle instead of trying to hold onto everything. J. and our children soar now, high above this place we call home, with freedom I can only imagine.

My mind returned to a poem I received by e-mail from a friend, not long after the accident. I had printed it and hung the paper on my refrigerator. Its words from the book, *The Leaning Tree,* touched me from the moment I read them for the first time.

Faith

When we walk to the edge of all the light we have
and take that step into the darkness of the unknown,
we must believe that one of two things will happen –

There will be something solid for us to stand on,
or, we will be taught how to fly.

Patrick Overton © 1975

That happened to me. I came to a time of complete darkness in my life. By faith, I stepped out into the unknown, expecting there to be something on which to stand. As I fell, God taught me how to fly. When I needed rest, He lifted me up with his eagles' wings. Eventually, with lots of practice, I learned to soar.

". . . those who hope in the LORD will renew their strength. They will soar on wings like eagles; they will run and not grow weary, they will walk and not be faint."[93]

Chapter 19

FOR GOD'S GLORY

"The Lord himself goes before you and will be with you; he will never leave you nor forsake you. Do not be afraid; do not be discouraged."

DEUTERONOMY 31:8

How does one end the story of a heart that is still beating?

If I could, I would make you a cup of tea and invite you into my living room for a chat. I'd listen to your story, and let you ask questions of mine. We would cry, and laugh, and talk to God together about the things that puzzle us.

Every day, we take a few more steps down the path of our lives. We have no way of knowing what lies ahead, or around the bend. If we spend our lives worrying about what might happen, we won't enjoy the flowers on the edge of the path, nor see the beautiful sunset off to the west. The joy must be in the journey.

Not everything that happens along the way is joyous. No, sometimes the path gets dark and lonely, or even frightening. But we have the opportunity to have a companion on that path who has promised to never leave us. No one else loves us like He does. Nor does anyone else have the power to sustain us like our Creator.

He knows me so well. That's why He uses both story and song to speak to me.

The words of a song stick in my brain, sometimes even annoyingly. If you start humming the theme song for Gilligan's Island, it will be in my mind for hours. But likewise, if I awake with a song from the Lord on my mind, I'll ponder it all day. It's important for me to choose carefully what music I listen to because my mind will faithfully record it. That's probably why God sang, "This is for my glory,"[94] instead of speaking it. I might have forgotten it otherwise.

I hope you will take the time to find a Christian music station you enjoy and listen to it. But it's ok if God speaks to you in a different way. God knows all of His children. He will find a way to communicate with you. Tune your ears to listen.

Nothing can clear the cobwebs of my mind better than a story. That's why God often uses Biblical stories to teach me about Himself. Throughout this book, I shared some of those lessons with you. The story of the widow burying her only son opened my eyes to God's compassion for me. David taught me to remember what God did in the past, and thus trust He has the power to do mighty works in the present. In the book of Esther, I learned how to find meaning in my current life through my daily relationship with God. When I read about Naomi accepting God's gift of Ruth, I finally saw God's gift of a daughter and son standing right in front of me.

But those stories are just the tip of the iceberg. There are hundreds of stories in the Bible—and they are all true life stories. I hope you will choose to spend some time reading them. It is God's words to us for today. Even though the words and stories have been around for centuries, their truths are still current. The more time I spend there, the more I understand God's character. Remember J.'s Bible Reading Plan is on my website. I invite you to follow the plan to begin reading.

This simple, ordinary woman has seen God display his miraculous power.

So. Can. You.

This book is part of my true life story. But mine is not any more important than yours to God. I hope you will invite him to display his miraculous power in your story too—and be willing to share those stories with others.

My wounded heart found hope and healing in the tender touch of my Savior. There is no greater display of God's miraculous power than a hope-filled life, especially in the face of great loss.

Hope waits for you too. His name is Jesus. He's the one who can teach your heart to sing again.

Come to Jesus
Come to Jesus and live[95]

Acknowledgments

I'm quite certain I could not have written this book without the help of a holy army of people, each lending me their skills and strengthening me with their prayers.

Rita Thomas, I would have never started writing if you hadn't contacted me with a message from God. Thank you for listening to Him and prodding me forward, both to write, and to go to Blue Ridge Mountain Christian Writers Conference. There I met so many people who encouraged me and believed in me—thank you, Cyle Young, Linda Gilden, Katy Kaufman, Jake McCandless, and a multitude of new friends from BRMCWC 2017.

Only Carol Russell would have the patience to help an old friend make an outline for a book after it's already written. You taught me a great deal about writing and helped me take a group of stories to a book. I'm so grateful.

Pamela Clements, you may not realize how significantly God used you to encourage me. When I got mixed up and e-mailed you accidentally, your kind response changed my pathway. You believed in my writing and my story and pointed me to the woman who became my editor and agent, Ami McConnell.

Ami, I truly believe God simply gave you a love for my story. Your tender heart for the Lord's leading blessed my soul and opened doors of opportunity. Your connections led me to remarkable people I never would have met as an unknown, first-time author, including my fabulous line editor, Karli Jackson and my gifted publisher, David Hancock.

David and the team at Morgan James Publishing are amazing. They treated me with kindness and patience, even though I knew almost nothing about publishing. Throughout the process, I knew I was surrounded by a team who not only were qualified, but also would tenderly lead me through the unknown territory ahead of me.

There are so many more to thank. You know who you are—those who asked the hard questions and gave tough answers, those who sent me pencils to remind me to write, those who didn't let me give up even when I sputtered tears all over their shoulder, those who took me away so I could rest beside the lake, and those that covered me with prayer.

I am deeply grateful and indebted to those of you who are in the pages of this book. You graciously gave me permission to tell our story even though it cost your heart for me to share. We have walked through deep pain together and will continue to do so until the day we enter the gates of heaven and leave all sorrow behind.

Janessa, Jayden, and J. L., words cannot express my thankfulness for the years I spent with you, nor can they express my anticipation to see you again. Watching the sky, ready to fly . . .

Which leads me to the One to whom I owe the deepest gratitude. I humbly kneel before You once again to say thank you, God—for my life.

ARMY
ONE

About the Author

PHOTO BY BRANDI STAPLETON

Lora Jones was born and raised on a farm near Liberal, Kansas. She earned an accounting degree from Kansas State University in 1986, but the best part of K-State was meeting her future husband, J. L. Jones. They married in 1985, and then furthered their education together at Midwestern Baptist Theological Seminary, completing their degrees in 1989. With school finally behind them, the young couple soon celebrated the birth of two children, Janessa and Jayden. Living in three states over their twenty years of marriage, J. L. and Lora served the Lord in full-time ministry until tragedy struck the family in 2004. An automobile accident claimed the lives of the entire family—except Lora.

With nothing left of her former life, Lora began the long journey toward finding hope.

Today, Lora Jones is an inspirational speaker. Weaving the stories of Biblical characters with her own life story, she encourages others to renew their faith in God even in difficult circumstances. Her storytelling style enables her to communicate with people of differing backgrounds and denominations, and to audiences of all sizes. For more information, or to schedule Lora to speak at your church, retreat, or event, go to www.lorajones.org.

Lora returned to her hometown, Liberal, Kansas, in 2007 to be closer to her extended families. She enjoys quiet mornings in her study chair with a cup of hot tea, long talks with good friends, and traveling across the country sharing the hope of Jesus to wounded hearts.

Notes

PREFACE:

1. John Mark Hall and Steven Curtis Chapman, "Voice of Truth" (Nashville: Capitol CMG Publishing, 2003).

CHAPTER 1:

2. Ibid.
3. Ibid.
4. Ibid.
5. Ibid.
6. Ibid.
7. Stuart K. Hine, "How Great Thou Art" (Carol Stream: Hope Publishing, 1949, 1953).
8. Ibid.
9. Ibid. Italics added for emphasis.

CHAPTER 2:

10. John Mark Hall and Steven Curtis Chapman, "Voice of Truth."
11. Mary B. C. Slade, "Footsteps of Jesus" (1871).
12. Ibid.

CHAPTER 3:

13. Connie S. Owens, Comfort in the Mourning, (Grief Recovery Services, 2002).
14. Ibid.
15. Ibid.

16. Will L. Thompson, "Jesus is All the World to Me" (1904).
17. Ibid.
18. Hebrews 11:1-12:3
19. Connie S. Owens, Comfort in the Mourning.
20. Hebrews 11:1
21. I Corinthians 7:17, 20, & 24

CHAPTER 4:

22. Connie S. Owens, Comfort in the Mourning.
23. Ibid.
24. Bart Millard, "Homesick" (Essential Music Publishing, 2004).
25. Ibid.

CHAPTER 5:

26. Connie S. Owens, Comfort in the Mourning.
27. John Mark Hall and Steven Curtis Chapman, "Voice of Truth."
28. Ibid.
29. Beth Redman and Matt Redman, "Blessed Be Your Name" (Nashville: Capitol CMG Publishing, 2005).
30. Ibid.
31. Ibid.
32. Ibid.
33. Ibid.
34. Ibid.

CHAPTER 6:

35. Chris Rice, "Untitled Hymn" (WB Music Corp, 2003).
36. Ibid.
37. Ibid.
38. Ibid.
39. Ibid.
40. Ibid.
41. Ibid.
42. Numbers 19:11-13

CHAPTER 7:

43. Ginny Owens and Kyle David Matthews, "If You Want Me To" (Nashville: Capitol CMG Publishing, 1999).
44. Ibid.
45. Ibid.

CHAPTER 8:

46. I Samuel 16
47. I Samuel 17:33-37
48. I Samuel 10:23
49. I Samuel 17
50. I Samuel 18-31
51. II Samuel 2:4; 5:1-5

CHAPTER 9:

52. Gloria Gaither and William J. Gaither, "The Church Triumphant" (Nashville: Capitol CMG Publishing, 2009).
53. Ibid.

CHAPTER 10:

54. Connie S. Owens, Comfort in the Mourning.
55. James Bryson, Nathan Cochran, Barry Graul, Pete Kipley, Bart Millard, Mike Sheuchzer, and Robby Shaffer, "Unaware" (Essential Music Publishing, 2004).
56. Ibid.
57. Robert Munsch and Sheila McGraw, Love You Forever, (Firefly Books Ltd., 1987).
58. Ibid.
59. Connie S. Owens, Comfort in the Mourning.
60. Luke 8:45b
61. Luke 8:46
62. Connie S. Owens, Comfort in the Mourning.
63. Ibid.
64. John Mark Hall and Steven Curtis Chapman, "Voice of Truth."

CHAPTER 11:

65. Connie S. Owens, Comfort in the Mourning.
66. John Mark Hall, "Who Am I?" (Nashville: Capitol CMG Publishing, 2003).
67. Ibid.

CHAPTER 12:

68. Story from Esther 1-2
69. Story from Esther 3-4
70. Connie S. Owens, Comfort in the Mourning.
71. Story from Esther 5:1-4
72. Story from Esther 5-7
73. Esther 8:1-2

CHAPTER 13:

74. John Mark Hall, "Lifesong" (Nashville: Capitol CMG Publishing, 2005).
75. Ibid.

CHAPTER 14:

76. Katherine Hankey and William G. Fischer, "I Love to Tell the Story" (1866, 1869).
77. Ibid.
78. Ibid.
79. Ibid.

CHAPTER 16:

80. Elizabeth C. Clephane, "The Ninety and Nine" (1868).
81. Ibid.

CHAPTER 17:

82. Story from Ruth 1-4
83. Bernie Herms and Nichole Nordeman, "I'm With You (Ruth and Naomi)" (Nashville: Capitol CMG Publishing, 2011).
84. Ibid.
85. Ibid.

CHAPTER 18:

86. Katharina A. von Schlegel, "Be Still, My Soul" (1752). Translated by Jane L. Borthwick, (1855).
87. Ibid.
88. Ibid.
89. Ibid.
90. Story from Mark 4:35-41
91. Beth Redman and Matt Redman, "Blessed Be Your Name."
92. Katharina A. von Schlegel and Jane L. Borthwick, "Be Still, My Soul."
93. Isaiah 40:31

CHAPTER 19:

94. John Mark Hall and Steven Curtis Chapman, "Voice of Truth."
95. Chris Rice, "Untitled Hymn."

FOR THE + DEVELOPING WORLD
LIBRARY
FOR ALL
DIGITAL LIBRARY + + +

Morgan James makes all of our titles available through the Library for All Charity Organization.

www.LibraryForAll.org

Printed in the USA
CPSIA information can be obtained
at www.ICGtesting.com
JSHW022336140824
68134JS00019B/1514

9 781642 792201